BURNTISLAND
Fife's Railway Port
by
Peter Marshall

High Street, Burntisland

THE OAKWOOD PRESS

© Oakwood Press & Peter Marshall 2001

British Library Cataloguing in Publication Data
A Record for this book is available from the British Library
ISBN 0 85361 578 0

Typeset by Oakwood Graphics.
Repro by Ford Graphics, Ringwood, Hants.
Printed by Inkon Printers Ltd, Yateley, Hants.

A 1960s view of the booking office and waiting room for ferry passengers at Burntisland. The sign on the canopy reads 'GRANTON-BURNTISLAND FERRY, BOOKING OFFICE, PAY HERE'. *A.A. Maclean*

Title page: Burntisland High Street 1879. *St Andrews University Library/JV 1721*

Front cover: The West Dock, Burntisland after the opening of the new East Dock.
Douglas Yuill Collection
Rear cover, top: Sketch drawing of the new West Dock in 1876.
Burntisland Heritage Trust
Rear cover, bottom: ScotRail class '150' on a Fife Circle service crosses the Links at Burntisland, October 2000. *Author*

Published by The Oakwood Press (Usk), P.O. Box 13, Usk, Mon., NP15 1YS.
E-mail: oakwood-press@dial.pipex.com
Website: www.oakwood-press.dial.pipex.com

Contents

Chapter One	Progress as a Port	5
Chapter Two	The Edinburgh & Northern Railway	15
Chapter Three	The Edinburgh, Perth & Dundee Railway	47
Chapter Four	The North British Railway	65
Chapter Five	Harbour Developments	79
Chapter Six	The Twentieth Century	111
Chapter Seven	Industrial Railways of the District	157
Appendix One	Locomotives of the E&NR and EP&DR	175
Appendix Two	Coal Shipments through Burntisland	177
Appendix Three	Ferry Revenue 1835 to 1838	179
Appendix Four	Mineral Wagons Observed at Burntisland in 1880	181
Appendix Five	Boats on the Burntisland Crossing	184
Appendix Six	Chronology	187
	Acknowledgements	189
	Bibliography	190
	Index	191

The viaduct over Harbour Place, Burntisland, with a class '150' leaving for Aberdour, October 2000.   *Author*

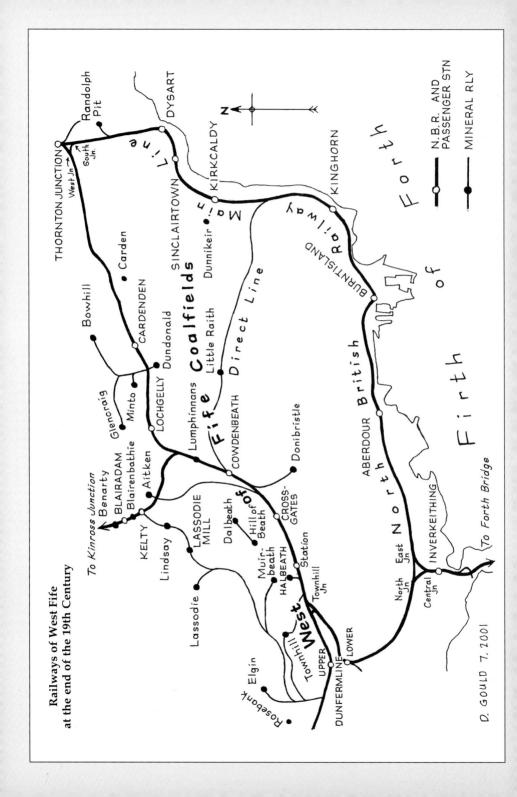

Railways of West Fife
at the end of the 19th Century

D. GOULD 7. 2001

Chapter One

Progress as a Port

Historical Background

The town of Burntisland has a long history as a port for the Kingdom of Fife, due in no small measure to its sheltered situation on the northern shores of the Firth of Forth on the East Coast of Scotland. Julius Agricola and his Roman army are believed to have crossed the river from the south near present day Granton in 83 AD, as they marched into the unfamiliar territory of northern Scotland to fight at the battle of Mons Graupius. Behind the settlement, to the north-west, lies Dunearn Hill, rising almost 700 feet above sea level, which was believed to have been a Pictish fort, defended unsuccessfully against the Romans. The occupying Roman forces called the port *Portis Gratiae*.

Initially known as Kinghorn Waster (or Wester), the earliest settlement of Burntisland was neither an island nor burned, but a fishing hamlet, providing food for the inhabitants of Rossend castle nearby and forming part of the barony of Kinghorn. King James IV built what was reputed to be the largest ship in the world at that time, *Michael*, often referred to as *Great Michael*. The ship is believed to have been built at Newhaven, across the Forth, it is just possible that some work was done in Burntisland, and certainly the ship paid several visits to the port before being sold to the King of France in 1514.

In 1540, during the reign of King James V, Robert Orrock was recorded as being 'maister of the works of Brint Eland for trymmen, irn and making stane boit' (the dry dock). Its maritime history never far from the surface, the town was sometimes referred to as 'portis salutis'. The King recognised the advantage of the safe harbour and, in 1541, persuaded the Abbey of Dunfermline to exchange it for a parcel of land.

Mary, Queen of Scots, is reputed to have lodged in Rossend Castle, Burntisland, on her way to St Andrew's. The night was proved eventful, for Chatelard, a Frenchman of her court who was overwhelmed with love for the Queen, attempted to conceal himself in her room but was soon discovered by the indignant monarch. In awarding the town the status of royal burgh in 1568, her son James VI effectively made the town independent from Kinghorn, its eastern neighbour.

The town seal showed a three-masted vessel, sails furled, at sea with flag flying and two mariners on deck. The motto was '*Sigillum Burgi de Burntisland*'. Fish were depicted on the reverse with the dictum 'Success to the Herring Fishing'. Fighting ships were based at the port to fend off any possible attack from the Spanish Armada in the 1580s or, later, the Huguenots in the 1620s, but its naval importance declined with the rise of Leith on the southern shore. In order to avoid crossing the Forth in stormy conditions, James VI ordered the entire General Assembly of the Church of Scotland to meet him at the church in Burntisland in 1601. The meeting had great significance for it was at the Burntisland meeting that the King James' version, a translation of the Bible associated with his name, was approved.

Gifts for Charles I's Coronation were loaded on a small baggage ferry when the king visited Scotland in 1633. However, on 10th July, in a typical Forth squall, the ferry sank off Burntisland, as it was *en route* to load the silver plate, jewels coins and other gifts on the *Dreadnought*. The sinking was hushed up as the loss of more than 30 noblemen and sailors as well as the gifts was considered a bad omen for the king. In 1992, the treasure became the subject of a search of the river and the town's Heritage Trust mounts summer exhibitions showing progress.

In the middle of the 17th century, Cromwell crossed the river as he moved his men northwards into Fife, strengthening his grip on Scotland after the battle of Dunbar in September 1650. The Parliamentarian troops are believed to have encamped at Lammerlaws, a rocky promontory on the shoreline. The impact of military forces occupying Burntisland was said to have had a detrimental effect on the local economy during the army's nine-year stay, from which the burgh was still recovering 30 years later.

The town showed an independent spirit when it held out against Cromwell and demanded that he repair the roads and quays in the town. It is not certain whether Cromwell's men actually carried out the task themselves, but he did contribute £30 to the work. He was impressed with Burntisland as a port for he wrote to his secretary, John Milton, in 1651 that the town was the 'best port in these parts'. In a further letter dated 29th July, 1651 to the Speaker of the House of Commons, he described Burntisland as, 'marvellous, capable of improvement in that respect without great charge, with a harbour a fathom deeper than at Leith at high spring tide, and not commanded by any ground without the town'.

Further military occupation followed in the 18th century. In 1715, the year of the first Jacobite uprising, the rebellious Earl of Mar occupied the town, poised to make an assault on the capital, and during the later Jacobite uprising in 1746, Hessian troops were temporarily stationed in Burntisland.

The rich agricultural hinterland to the port produced good crops of cereals, but it was the sea which brought fortune back to Burntisland in the form of fish. Herring appeared in the Forth in large shoals in the final years of the 18th century and created work for many of the townsmen. The wealth which followed them was, of course, not simply in fishing but also in the associated industries such as barrel making, fish curing and ship building. The latter was responsible for many of the 500 boats that were reported to have been found in the port by the beginning of the 19th century.

The abundance of fish was apparent from a contemporary advertisement in Dunfermline for salt and red herrings. Available from George Lauder, (uncle of Andrew Carnegie) they were available in full and half barrels at 2*d*. and 3*d*. per dozen. It seemed unnecessary for the advertisement to point out that 'this is very cheap'. However, the fish were fickle and by the 1830s, their numbers had depleted to such an extent that, within only a few of years, a drop in the population of 300 had been recorded. The whisky distillery and the lime works once more became the focus of industry in Burntisland. Coal was exported from Fife ports by coasting and foreign vessels up to the 17th century.

Trade through the Fife ports had, however, declined after the Union of the Parliaments in 1707, when higher taxes drove traffic to new sea routes and, by the beginning of the 19th century, even fishing and whaling interests were

Outlook of Burntisland in 1693.   *Edward Wilson Collection*

moving away from the area. Chemicals soon became significant and, although an old established vitriol works had disappeared by the 1830s, a shale oil enterprise set up at Binnend in the 1880s employed up to 1,000 miners. However, it was coal mining, or rather the exporting of coal mined in the West Fife coal field, which gave Burntisland its wealth, bringing with it shipbuilding and then aluminium in the 20th century. There was some irony in this fact for Burntisland had been denied coal measures of its own, most possibly through the volcanic activity in the area that destroyed the rich deposits along that part of the Forth coastline. Throughout this time, however, it has been the port, which held the key to prosperity.

Dunearn is an extinct volcano and a lochan in the crater provided fresh water for the locality including a distillery was established in 1786 at Grange on the outskirts of Burntisland by Messrs Young and Company. James Stuart, a later proprietor of Dunearn House, was killed in 1822 in a duel with Sir Alexander Boswell, the son of Dr Johnson's biographer, James Boswell.

Early Communication Routes

The first recorded public conveyance between the Forth and the Tay was in 1805 when 'a two horse diligence . . . ran with much deliberation and leisure between Newport and Pettycur by Kennoway - a journey which generally occupied a whole day'. This statement was made in *Tullis's Guide to the Edinburgh and Northern Railway* of 1848 and, although probably an oversimplification, indicates the dearth of a regular service before this time. In 1810, Alexander McNab, owner of a hotel in Cupar, established a four-horse coach between the ferries and 'set about improving them'. Until the arrival of the railways, a number of coaches plied across the county, exhibiting such imposing names as *Thane of Fife*, *Maggie Lauder* and *Balcarries*.

So great was the improvement in coaching services that, in September 1834, Cupar district trustees of the turnpike allowed McNab a reduction in tolls because of the increase in traffic generated by his *Royal Union*, *Kingdom of Fife* and *Tally-ho* coaches. The route between Edinburgh and Aberdeen had largely been diverted away from the sometimes-treacherous Queensferry Passage and the road to Perth to the route through Fife from the harbour at Pettycur round the coast towards Cupar. Alternative travel developed with the fast steamboats that sailed directly from Dundee to Leith and even from Kirkcaldy to Leith at a fare of not much more than the ferry dues. It only required the inevitable arrival of the railway for the population to benefit from further improvement in travel.

Despite the river being around five miles wide at Pettycur, a ferry of sorts had crossed from the southern shore to Fife for centuries. The broad ferry plied from either Leith or Newhaven in about an hour, but if the weather was bad, the passage could take as long as five or six hours in a four-man sloop. The Queensferry crossing of the Forth upstream at the island of Inchgarvie received its royal connection through Queen Margaret, wife of King Malcolm Canmore, in the 11th century. The town of Dunfermline in Fife was the king's capital and so Margaret's use of the crossing to both Dunfermline and St Andrew's attached her name to the passage across the river. Although the Queensferry was a narrower crossing, the convenience of Burntisland, Pettycur and Aberdour for travellers to Edinburgh had made them more attractive passages.

By the end of the 18th century, consideration was being given to improving the Forth crossings. The Reverend James Wemyss, writing his report for the Old Statistical Account of Scotland, indicated that Cromwell had built the streets and quays of Burntisland but that the streets had not been improved since. He wrote: 'There is every reason to hope that they will soon be put into better condition as the gentlemen of the county have lately proposed to make a public ferry to cross from Burntisland to Newhaven, where it is intended to build a pier, in order to secure a passage for travellers passengers at any time of the tide'.

Commenting on the standard of housing, the Reverend Wemyss remarked on the availability of stone. 'There is a very fine quarry of free stone, a small distance north from the town, on the Grange estate. Most of the new buildings along the coast, to a considerable distance, are furnished with hewn work from that quarry. About a mile to the eastward, and also to the westward, there are inexhaustible quarries of limestone, which is sent off in great quantities to the works at Carron, and other places.'

Previous times had seen Acts in 1669 and 1686 giving powers to local justices of the peace and commissioners of supply to visit ferries and regulate them. However, the several ferry crossings vied with each other for trade and many corrupt practices grew up. In 1758, a committee was established to examine the 'irregularities and disorderly practices' that had crept in to the use of the ferries over the Forth. Acts of Parliament in 1792 and 1813, bringing with them fixed charges and improvements at Pettycur (near Kinghorn) and Burntisland, regulated the various ferries that traversed the river.

The Act 'for improving the communication between Edinburgh and Fife', which was passed in 1792, admitted that it was easier to cross to Burntisland with its sheltered harbour than either Kirkcaldy or Pettycur both of which were open to the vagaries of the North Sea. The recognition of Burntisland as a public ferry was a significant aspect of the Act, but it also gave authority to improve the landing places on both sides of the firth and to fix charges, with tolls set at one penny per person and two pence for a horse. Sanction was given for borrowing up to £3,000 at five per cent for improvement works.

At Burntisland, a new pier costing £600 would be built to replace the one that had been built by Cromwell, with £500 for a new turnpike and £50 for a new light. Pettycur would equally have £600 spent on it. The turnpike was probably as significant to Burntisland as was a new pier, for the town had poor landward communications to the North and the East. A new road to Kinghorn would ensure that the turnpike route through Fife from the Tay would continue beyond Pettycur to Burntisland.

A report to the Convention of Royal Burghs of Scotland on 14th July, 1795 stated that the harbour at Burntisland was 15 acres Scots (or 20 acres English) and had a depth of 20 to 22 feet with an opening of 100 feet and a pier to the south. Sibbald, an engineer, added that the port handled 225 decked vessels and 108 boats, and employed 1,631 men (not including women and children) during the winter months, exporting 56,865 barrels of herring. Sir John Rennie, the engineer, gave a further report of the ferries in February 1808 which acknowledged that Pettycur was 'one of the worst harbours on the Forth', with capacity falling short of that at Burntisland. Despite being acknowledged as an unsurpassed location for the northern terminus of the crossing, Burntisland had not been given adequate resources to enable the port to develop.

By 1813, it was apparent that the amount spent on improvements was not enough to advance the port sufficiently. A further Act repealed some of the 1792 statute, enabling more money to be spent on the piers and the roads and establishing a quorum for attendance at the trustees meetings. More importantly, licences were issued to those who wished to ply for trade on the crossing. Burntisland was to have two new piers erected to the south of the harbour and to have road access to the east. Access to the west would have been over the beach. Pettycur was once more to benefit with either the lengthening of its pier or a new landing place. A later Act, in May 1826, increased the amount to be borrowed to £19,000 for Burntisland and included another £24,600 for expansion at Newhaven. In addition, the road to Kinghorn was authorised at £3,500.

An even greater engineer, Thomas Telford, prepared a subsequent report on the crossing between 1827 and 1828. He made observations of the frequency and duration for the three ports, Kirkcaldy, Pettycur and Burntisland. He observed that Burntisland frequently accommodated ferries which could not make harbour at the other two ports during stormy weather. During the period of his observations, only five crossings were cancelled at Burntisland against 51 at Kirkcaldy and 24 at Pettycur. He described the wind directions being mainly from south, south-east and south-west, commenting that gales, which blew from the north-east and the south-east, gave 'considerable sea' as far inshore as Queensferry. Telford was a strong supporter of Burntisland as the northern destination of the ferry, pointing out that Pettycur had no proper anchorage for vessels. He recommended a pier be built to the east of the harbour on the land belonging to both James Farnie and to Miss Charter. (Farnie owned the dry-dock.) He believed that the proposed road or even a railway to Kinghorn was desirable.

Leith, as the southern end of the broad ferry, was the port for Edinburgh and therefore was, in its own right, a flourishing community, which seldom seemed to have sufficient accommodation for shipping. Rennie put forward abortive plans in 1818 for new docks at nearby Newhaven. However, the famous chain pier was built at Newhaven and opened in 1822 by King George IV on his extended visit to Edinburgh, when he stayed with the then 16-year-old Duke of Buccleuch at Dalkeith. Sir Walter Scott was in charge of the festivities, which he planned to be a week-long celebration of Scottish culture, over which the king would set his seal of approval. The chain pier was to prove very popular with the travelling public and soon became known amongst locals as 'the baggage pier'.

The Burntisland Ferry

However, there was still no satisfactory service for the travelling public across the Forth and a later Act, the Burntisland and Granton Pier, Ferry and Road Act was passed to provide, amongst others things, a low water pier at Burntisland. While the Granton works began promptly, those at Burntisland were slow to commence and in 1837, George Smith, an engineer of 8 Wemyss Place, Edinburgh, was asked by James Farnie to produce a report on the best positions for a new slipway for the ferry at Burntisland. He confirmed the widely held opinion that Burntisland had decided advantages over the other ports for the location of a low water pier. He expressed surprise that the surveys undertaken by Sibbald in 1795, Sir John Rennie in 1809 and Thomas Telford in 1829 had not yet seen Burntisland 'fixed upon as the principal Ferry Station on the north of the Forth'.

Smith considered the inadequacy of Rennie's location for a pier and proposed that any extension to it would require a carriageway to pass behind the dry dock, which was situated at the eastern wall of the harbour. This would provide the least expensive and most direct route to the town. Construction could re-use stones from the present quayside walls and mud and clay dredged from the harbour would fill in behind the new wall and form the basis for the roadway. A drawbridge would be needed across the entrance to the dry dock. Smith's second suggestion was to erect the pier to the east of the harbour, thus avoiding the conflict of ferry movements with those of traffic for the harbour. His estimates for the two proposals were £12,400 and £11,870, respectively. In either instance, a new road to Kinghorn was essential and would cost an additional £2,050.

It was desirable for there to be only one location which had a 'communication' to the Tay Ferry, and Smith believed that Telford's estimates were high and that, if work could be done more cheaply, it would be in the national interest to proceed with a low water pier. Soundings had been taken and the best site was off the existing east landing slip on James Farnie's property at the port. A new road should be built over the several properties, which lay along the east of the harbour to the quayside to be formed at the low water pier. Here a powerful crane would be needed to load and unload vessels.

Cost remained an important consideration even contributing to delay and postponement, and Smith suggested that if dressed stone facings to the quay and pier proved to be too expensive then rough blocks would serve the same purpose. He hoped that the Trustees and the gentlemen of Fife would raise the sums required particularly for a good road to Pettycur. He observed that the low water pier at Granton 'is in a great state of forwardness' which should give powerful inducement to set about the works for Burntisland. A low water pier was essential to the quick turn round of steam-powered vessels, which were becoming the order of the day. Sailing boats could either wait for high tide or discharge passengers (and goods) into lighters, which would then take them ashore.

The existing piers were showing their age and were liable to damage from the storms, which are common on the firth. On 24th February, 1837, an easterly gale struck damaging most of the piers on that part of the river. At Burntisland a portion of the jetty was destroyed, as were the piers behind the Lammerlaws and at Lochies.

Yet another report was prepared in 1838 by James Leslie, a civil engineer from Dundee. Leslie was later consulted on other projects including, in 1845, the Dundee & Forfar Junction Railway, the first but unfulfilled proposal between the two towns. His report confirmed once more that Burntisland was the best landing place on the coast of Fife. Moreover, it was well situated for building materials with good freestone for ashlar blocks at Grange and Dalachy quarries nearby, the later offering both limestone and sandstone. Newbiggin quarry next door also yielded limestone. Leslie commented that Rennie's report had been written before the arrival of steamboats and so may be considered to be out of date. He noted that Burntisland had poor land access, with Binn Hill at 600 feet behind the town forming a natural barrier to the north. A new road to Perth had been built across the high ground about 1¼ miles to the west of Dunearn. There were steep inclines of between 1 in 12 and 1 in 14. The road from Tayport to Kirkcaldy and Kinghorn should be extended to Burntisland.

Leslie could not see how the ferry to Burntisland would attract passengers especially with the absence of any means of access by road to the port and industry or trade. The low water pier was good for those who wanted a short crossing, he believed, but there was insufficient trade for frequent crossings, which are required of a main or national port. Kirkcaldy had poor facilities for passengers with no shelter and no slipway, which could mean that, at low tide, embarkation at Kirkcaldy was somewhat primitive, taking place from the beach using a small, wheeled gangway. Pettycur was deemed to be expensive to operate since it was exposed and filled up easily. Old Kinghorn adjacent to Pettycur did have a sheltered outlook, but it too filled up with sand.

Burntisland on the other hand had little or no recorded silting as, at that time, the tide washed over the muddy river bottom. As if to emphasise the fast flowing nature of the river, Leslie pointed out that peat from Blair Drummond Moss, above Stirling, could be found at Leith. He contradicted his findings with a report that the harbour at Burntisland had filled up since the quay had been constructed (adjacent to the future railway station) in 1795, and was only 17 feet to 20 feet deep.

The first new pier was completed in 1838 and from that date the vessels that formed the Newhaven to Pettycur crossing transferred to Burntisland. The middle pier at Granton was partially opened on 28th June, 1838, providing a new departure point from the southern side of the river. The opening ceremony was held on the day of the coronation of Queen Victoria, and was performed in the Duke's absence by Lord John Scott, his brother, who named the pier 'Victoria Jetty' in honour of the young Queen. The Queen's first visit to Scotland

Burntisland Harbour in 1834, an engraving by Joseph Swan from a drawing by James Stewart in *Fife Illustrated* by John M. Leighton.   *St Andrews University Library*

'The Chain Pier at Newhaven around 1840' from an engraving by R. Brandard after W.H. Bartlett.   *Author's Collection*

Prince Albert Pier, Burntisland. *Kirkcaldy Museum 1986/440*

Map of Burntisland in 1854. *National Library of Scotland*

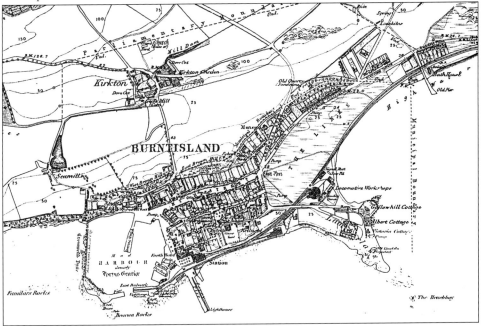

was her landing at the pier on 1st September, 1842, an unexpected arrival which caused the Edinburgh magistrates considerable consternation. The pier was thereafter opened unceremoniously by stages until completed in October 1844 and the new service introduced.

The replacement on the northern shore was named the 'Prince Albert' pier and opened at Burntisland on 5th September, 1844. The ferry was constituted under an Act of 15th September, 1844 and was operated first by sailing vessels and then with three second-hand steamers. The Act required the proprietors to provide, for twenty-five years, at least seven daily crossings for passengers and goods traffic between April and October, decreasing to six in the winter months, unless an act of God or other unavoidable incident occurred.

The distance crossed was reduced by about two miles when the ferry had transferred to the Granton and Burntisland route and the duration to between 35 and 45 minutes by sailing vessel and 25 minutes by steamer. From 1845, as the ferry grew in importance, the number of passengers crossing almost doubled from 115,000 to 210,000 in three years. One significant user of the ferry was John Young, the owner of the Grange distillery, who had branched into farming and took up to 700 head of cattle across the Forth annually.

Two leading landowners were appointed as trustees to ensure that the ferry did not decline into the poor standards of the past. The Duke of Buccleuch and John Gladstone (father of W. E. Gladstone) were responsible for the crossing and improving the harbours on both sides of the river. The Duke had spent £80,000 from his private means building the pier at Granton. A smaller sum (£37,000) was spent by Fife County Council, along with a contribution from Gladstone, on improving the facilities at Burntisland. The eventuality of a railway was foreseen in the 1842 Act, for a clause provided that 'in the event of a railway being . . . established through Fife, terminating at Burntisland, the said Duke and the said John Gladstone shall give every facility, the same with the said pier'. Gladstone employed several vessels on the passage, PS *Maid of Leven*, PS *Granton*, and PS *Burntisland*. He ordered the PS *Forth*, but the railway company took delivery of the vessel in February 1847.

The use of rail in the district to transport minerals was not new, since waggonways had existed in the district for some years to ease the transportation of minerals such as coal, lime and salt to the shores of the river. Coal masters sought methods of carrying the output of their mines from the West Fife coal measures to the shores of the River Forth and amongst the many waggonways that provided the required access were the Elgin and Halbeath near Dunfermline. A few miles to the west of Burntisland lay the Fordell Railway (which had been established in about 1770) and it, along with other colliery lines, will be covered in a later chapter. Thus, the scene was set for the arrival of the railway. The early developments had been undertaken in Northumberland, Lancashire and, in Scotland, at Glasgow, Edinburgh and Dundee. The steam engine as a means of power was improving and the nation had become gripped in the 'Railway Mania' of the mid-1840s. Railway lines had reached Scotland from London by this time and the next push was up the east coast to Aberdeen and to the Highlands. Only the deep indents of the firths of Forth and Tay stood in the way of a continuous line from South to North.

Chapter Two

The Edinburgh & Northern Railway

The first serious railway proposal associated with Burntisland was intended to run along the coast to Queensferry and the West Fife coalfield around Dunfermline, intersecting with the several waggonways which ran down to the Forth. The proposition, like others in the forthcoming years, fell on the wrong side of Burntisland town council. These august gentlemen refused permission for the line to cross the end of the High Street by means of a level crossing, a move that would have created an obstruction to the harbour. Instead, and ignoring all the advantages presented by steam power, they insisted that all transfers to and from the pier would have to be made under horsepower. In addition, charges for the movement of goods through the harbour were so steep as to put the scheme beyond the realms of practicality. Had they allowed the railway to be built, any transfer dues levied, like in so many other Scottish towns, would have provided the burgh of Burntisland with a good source of revenue.

Railways on the Southern Shore

On the southern shore of the River Forth, there was also uncertainty over the construction of a line. The first Bill was for a railway from Edinburgh to Leith and Newhaven, projected in 1835, and an Act was granted on 13th August, 1836 for the Edinburgh and Newhaven Railway. The line was originally laid out by Grainger and Miller, two of Scotland's best known engineers of their time. Capitalisation was underestimated at £100,000 and compensation claims from landowners put paid to the effectiveness of the project. Later the promoters of the Trinity pier took up the scheme.

The central Edinburgh station of the Edinburgh, Leith & Newhaven Railway (EL&NR) at Canal Street 'at a place known as Market Street in the Parish of the High Church' was difficult to reach. Rail movement at Canal Street (later Waverley) was made more awkward when the North British and the Edinburgh & Glasgow railways arrived at right angles from both the East and the West respectively requiring the EL&NR to cross these tracks. An expensive tunnel over 1,000 yards long also had to be constructed for the route to Newhaven, on a very steep gradient beneath the New Town, adding to the woes of the Directors. Once open, traffic through the tunnel was hauled by rope, a common feature of the time. Work on construction of the 2¼ mile line proceeded at a leisurely pace, during which time a battle within the EL&NR Boardroom led to a new Board being appointed in 1837. In 1839, with progress still slow, a new Act was sought to build the line onwards from Newhaven to the chain pier at Trinity. The extension opened on 31st August, 1842. Canal Street remained a separate station until 1868.

With Granton harbour nearing completion, the reformed company proposed to extend further its recently opened line to this new destination, receiving an Act for this portion on 19th July, 1844. In keeping with the final terminus, the Edinburgh, Leith & Granton Company (EL&GR) was the name taken by the railway on the southern shore. The North British Railway made an approach with the aim of amalgamation, however the EL&GR, like many other small companies of the time which sought the best outcome from amongst a number of suitors, deferred the decision. On Christmas Eve 1845, the company announced that it would wait until the intentions of the Caledonian Railway (CR) became clear.

The CR was approaching Edinburgh from the West and had plans for a line from Slateford to Granton, intending to obtain some of the trade from the port and divert it away from both the Edinburgh & Glasgow and the North British to its new line from Carstairs. Indeed, by March 1846, it had presented a Bill for such a line. The Edinburgh & Glasgow had designs on access to the Forth ports and possession of the EL&GR would provide an advantage over the Caledonian. The CR was given access from the head of the pier to the rails laid by the Duke on the pier itself.

The new pier at Granton was completed in October of that year and the railway's extension and passenger facilities were finished on 19th February, 1846, when the railhead became the new terminus for the Burntisland ferry. The station was originally located at the head of the pier, although on its completion it was moved 800 feet down the pier to the end so that passengers had only a short distance to walk. The new pier was considered a great improvement on the poor arrangements which had existed for some time at Leith. Shipping continued to sail from the Forth as it had done for years previously, departing from Granton to Dundee, Montrose and ports further up the East Coast of Scotland. The coastal trade presented the impending railway with stiff competition.

The EL&GR, however, needed the line through Fife to ensure its future. For many years prior to the coming of railways, the fires in Edinburgh's terraced Georgian houses had been supplied by coal from Cluny, Dundonald and Lochgelly in the West Fife coalfield, coal that attracted high prices in the capital. In addition, any short line running north from Edinburgh had to depend on the ferry traffic from Fife for its trade.

Formation of the Company

There had been several attempts in the early years of the 19th century to bring a line through Fife from Burntisland. The year 1819 saw Robert Stevenson, an Edinburgh civil engineer, propose a railway from Forth to Tay through the West Fife coalfield. Later, in 1835, the Earl of Rothes commissioned John Geddes to survey a route followed the next year by Robert Stevenson's second proposal, similar to his first, from Burntisland through Kirkcaldy and Cupar to Ferryport-on-Tay (later known as Tayport). Thomas Grainger and John Miller, well known Scots engineers, submitted an almost identical proposal also in 1836. The potential subscribers to a railway along the second route met in Cupar on 13th October, 1840 when those present included several businessmen with more than a passing interest in the projection of the railway through Fife:

James Tod and Sons, railway spring makers of Edinburgh
James Mitchell, railway contractors of Falkirk
Cuthbert and Sons, coach builders of Dundee
Peter Borrie, engineer of Dundee
John Wilson, Dundyvan Iron Works
Neil McDonald, railway contractors of Kilsyth
K. Martin, railway contractors of Kilsyth
John Marshall, railway contractor of Glasgow (who offered to take almost 30 shares)

Preliminary sums for Parliamentary surveys, plans, estimates and 'lodging copies with schoolmasters' were approved at a meeting at Cupar on 29th October, 1840. Shares were offered at £10 each, but a decision was taken to wait until the money market was more favourable before proceeding. Those gentlemen, who took preliminary shares, were to have preference in the 'Parliamentary' stock. £2,500 was required for Parliamentary preparations. Grainger and Miller themselves took £500 of preliminary stock and were appointed to be Engineers to the line.

Although the southern end of the route at Burntisland opposite to Edinburgh was never much in doubt, there were two northern objectives, Dundee and Perth, which left the promoters undecided about the line through Fife. An engineer, John Milne, contested Grainger's route in January 1841, believing that Perth was the best destination and proposed a route via Auchterderran and Loch Leven to Newburgh crossing the Tay to join the Dundee & Perth Railway. Both engineers produced figures to support their argument, Grainger rejecting Milne as of 'no experience whatsoever in the planning and execution of railways'. The protagonists for Perth wanted to submit both routes to an engineer of eminence to decide the best course.

This was not necessary as there was no support for Milne's plan and it withered in the recessions of the early 1840s. Another later scheme, the Fife and Perth Railway reached Parliament in 1843 but failed to pass committee because of incomplete plans.

It was not until 1844 that a Prospectus was issued to raise £800,000 and seek a Bill for Grainger's Edinburgh, Dundee & Northern Railway, although the name was shortened to Edinburgh & Northern Railway (E&NR) on 1st March that year. The E&NR Directors were not to be intimidated by the unimaginative Burntisland town council as others had been previously and fought against the imposition of penalising charges for the crossing from Granton.

At a meeting in the company offices at 30 Queen Street, Edinburgh on 7th November, 1844, a committee of management was set up, comprising:

Earl of Leven, of Melville House, Cupar	Chairman
John Gladstone of Fasque by Fettercairn	Joint Deputy Chairman
Captain Ramsay, RN of Darnaway Street, Edinburgh	Joint Deputy Chairman
John Learmonth, Dean, 6 Moray Place, Edinburgh	
William Fullerton Lindsay Carnegie, of Boysack, Angus	

Sir John Richardson, Bart of Pitfour Castle, Perth
John Balfour, Balbirnie by Markinch
Earl of Glasgow
Edward Ellice, MP of Glenquoich, Invergarry
James A. Cheyne, Kilmaran, 55 Moray Place, Edinburgh
Tyndale Bruce of Falkland
John Gibson Junior, WS of Charlotte Street, Edinburgh
Archibald Home, accountant, 74 George Street, Edinburgh
John Thomson, Royal Bank of Scotland

Many of the names were committed Scots railway promoters. Carnegie was the Chairman of the Arbroath & Forfar Railway in Angus, and was a significant figure in the promotion of railways in that county. John Learmonth was active in both railway management and carriage construction. Lord Provost of Edinburgh between 1831 and 1833, he had been introduced to John Gladstone by the Duke of Buccleuch and seen the possibility of a tie-up between the North British Railway (NBR) and a line promoted through Fife. However, his allegiances lay with a line which was not the E&NR. In 1843, he had encouraged the NB's shareholders to invest in the potential Direct Northern Railway although there was no serious interest and the scheme did not even attain a Parliamentary deposit.

He had been so certain of the potential of the proposal that he had purchased the Halbeath waggonway for the Edinburgh & Perth Railway, expecting it to be a lucrative feeder line, but also in an attempt to hold the E&NR hostage. Now there was another scheme to the north and, with Learmonth's backing, it would give the Edinburgh & Northern a serious challenge. Certainly, with the breadth of his railway interests, Learmonth deserved his nickname of the 'Scottish Hudson'.

As chairman of the promoters of the Edinburgh & Perth Railway (E&PR), Learmonth was effectively promoting a contrary proposal at the same time as he was promoting the E&NR. He publicly declared that he was in favour of 'giving up organising a branch to Ferryport-on-Craig' on the Edinburgh & Northern Railway and instead wished to see his line made to Perth with a branch to Cupar. The latter idea was not taken up but the opposition of the Edinburgh & Perth Railway made life difficult for the E&NR for the next two years. The upstart line was intended to commence on the NBR's ally, the Edinburgh & Glasgow Railway (E&GR), of which Learmonth was the Chairman, and take the direct route to Perth via Queensferry.

The Edinburgh & Perth Railway fiercely fought the authorisation of the E&NR, but it failed to achieve approval for its own line in 1846. The E&PR returned to Parliament in 1847 with another proposal for a line from the E&GR and a branch to the West Fife coalfield. After a second attempt to seek authorisation, the E&PR failed but not before the Edinburgh & Northern had extracted some guarantees over further branch lines in West Fife, of which a little more later. The NBR made an early approach to the E&NR in November 1845, offering shares in a ratio of 11 NBR to nine E&NR. The offer was rejected by the E&NR Board who in turn suggested one £25 NBR for each £24 E&NR share. It was to be almost 20 years before the E&NR fell to the NBR ambitions.

John Gladstone declared himself to be 'seriously engaged in promoting the making of a Rail Road across Fife' and became the largest shareholder in the E&NR, taking £39,000 of stock, with the Duke of Buccleuch also acquiring a substantial share holding. Gladstone, who has been described as 'indomitable, assertive and quarrelsome', made his money in Liverpool where he had associations with the West Indies and the slave trade. He had been involved with the development of railways from their inception, being on the provisional committee of the Liverpool and Manchester Railway in 1824. His main investment was in the Grand Junction Railway in which he had over half of his £170,000 tied up, much of the rest enabling him to be the largest shareholder in the coal railways of Lanarkshire. With money also tied up in the Forth and Clyde Canal, his support for communications in central Scotland could not be called into question.

The Duke of Buccleuch, on the other hand, was the largest landowner in Scotland and had several residences one of which, Caroline Park overlooked the harbour at Granton. Like many landowners, the Duke was anxious to improve his property and thereby his income from it. He gave upwards of £500,000 through the years to improving the port facilities and so the ferry benefited from his wish to encourage more traffic across the river.

Ambitious Plan

The company had ambitious plans to gain the monopoly in Fife and to repel all assailants from the West. The determined route for the Edinburgh and Northern Railway was from the harbour at Burntisland to Kirkcaldy and Markinch. Onwards to Kettle a branch to Cupar would then be built, the main line continuing to Collessie and Newburgh, crossing the River Tay there and joining the Dundee & Perth Railway (D&PR) before entering Perth by means of that company's rails. This meant that traffic from Edinburgh to the North-East of Scotland could be sent via Perth by either the Scottish Midland Junction Railway (SMJR) or the D&PR. Included was a short but steeply inclined branch from Newburgh to the harbour on the Tay, while other proposals included a line from Ladybank to Kinross, and another from Markinch to the village of Leslie.

Southbound traffic would be directed over the Tay from Dundee to Newport and then over the turnpike to Cupar to join the railway. A further extension of the Cupar branch was clearly called for and this was proposed, along with others, to St Andrews and through the Lochgelly coalfield to Dunfermline, secured when the E&PR Bill failed. A later plan for a line from Lochgelly direct to Kirkcaldy was considered unnecessary and rejected. There was an oversight in drafting the Bill for the Dunfermline branch, for section 16 omitted the word 'coal' from the range of commodities to be carried, effectively restricting the major source of revenue! This was remedied just before Royal Assent with the inclusion of the word and of the rates of carriage. The terms were, a maximum of 1d. per ton per mile if carried over six miles and 2d. per ton per mile if below six miles.

Thomas Grainger declared, in a report dated 21st April, 1845, that a proposed Lochgelly branch would pass near the blast furnaces which were about to be built for the Lochgelly ironstone, coal from the immediate seams being estimated to provide 250,000 tons per year for the next 250 years. Ironstone was found within the coal seams at Lochgelly and the Lochgelly Iron and Coal Company sold the resultant pig iron as a by-product of coal mining. In his report, Grainger went on to point out that a bridge over the Tay at Ferryport-on-Craig would cost £164,000 and would make the branch line two miles shorter than a crossing at Newport, which was 14 miles from Cupar. The bridge would reduce the distance via Perth by another 16 miles. He also reckoned that the branch to Newburgh harbour would cost £10,000 although no survey was conducted. The branch to St Andrews would cost £30,000 for the four-mile route.

A scheme for a route from Perth to Crieff along the Almond Valley was supported by the E&NR, which offered to lease the line, to prevent the Scottish Central Railway (SCR) from procuring its coal traffic. £300,000 was to be raised for additional works and a projected nine per cent return was expected, for it was claimed that the coal to be found in Fife was equalled only by that in Lanarkshire.

An important concession was extracted from both Kinghorn and Kirkcaldy in May 1845 when the company was permitted to carry goods through the burghs, exempt from petty customs dues. More significant were the settlements reached with the important landowners of the district. The Earl of Rosslyn, who owned considerable land near Kirkcaldy, was paid £10,000 for 'land amenity and intersectional damage'. The damage to his estate was considered less detrimental than that to his neighbour, the Earl of Wemyss, for an additional payment would have to be made if the line was carried further north to avoid his land.

The Edinburgh and Northern Railway Company Bill passed on 11th June and the company was incorporated on 31st July, 1845, (8 & 9 Vict. cap. clviii). The Act enabled the construction of a railway, 'commencing at the low water pier at Burntisland, and terminating on the one hand at Perth and on the other at Cupar, with a short branch to the harbour of Kirkcaldy.' The promoters had sought authorisation for the route to be composed of a single track throughout with suitable passing places. The pressure of the Railway Mania on available capital had persuaded them to build their line as cheaply as possible. However, Parliament with an eye to the future had insisted that the railway be built with double track and the financial burden that this placed upon the company was to become apparent in forthcoming years.

The company was also anxious to tap into the West Fife coalfield, which was already exporting coal to Edinburgh. At first the E&PR offered to withdraw its opposition to the Edinburgh & Northern's Dunfermline branch if the latter would agree to its line through Fife. The E&NR Board's response was that the idea 'could not be entertained'. The E&NR compromised by agreeing not to oppose the E&PR proposal on condition that it could submit its own plan for a Lochgelly and Dunfermline branch, should the Edinburgh & Perth line be rejected. Fortunately for the E&NR, the tradesmen of Dunfermline supported the Northern company's plans for a branch to their town, assisting the downfall of the E&PR Bill. As an added assurance that the territory was firmly in the grip of the E&NR, a branch from Dunfermline to North Queensferry was agreed with the Stirling and Dunfermline company. The scheme was later withdrawn in order to reduce cost.

The first meeting of the E&NR Directors was held at the company offices on Monday 6th August, 1845. The attendance could hardly have been called enthusiastic, since only John Gibson, who was the Duke of Buccleuch's law agent, and John Thomson, an accountant from the Royal Bank of Scotland, were present to open the proceedings along with Thomas Grainger, the Engineer. Alexander Thomson, John Learmonth, Robert Landale and Captain Ramsay all arrived late! A copy of the Act was laid on the table and elections to office took place. Learmonth was elected Chairman of the Edinburgh & Northern, a move that offered a hint at the future direction which ownership of the company would take, and Ramsay retained his position as Vice Chairman. Learmonth was already the Chairman of the North British Railway (as well as the E&GR) and his latest appointment tightened his grip on central Scotland's railways.

The position of Secretary was given to Henry Lees, at an annual salary of £500, the Directors awarding themselves an allowance of £600 per annum. Grainger was given the task of advising on the management of the various departments and the appropriate salaries to be paid. A man with many demands on his expertise, he was to be paid only for the time that he spent on the company's business at a rate of £5 5s. per day, his principal assistant to be paid £1 11s. 6d. per day, other assistants at £1 1s. per day.

Construction Begins

Once the E&NR Act was confirmed, there was no delay in getting down to business for, on 13th August, 1845, tenders were invited for the construction of the first section of line, that from Burntisland to Kinghorn. Advertisements were placed in 23 publications, intimating that tenders would be opened on 24th September. The whole of the initial route was divided into nine contracts:

Burntisland	5,000 yards from the low water pier at Burntisland to Abden farm, east of Kinghorn
Invertiel	4,400 yards from Abden farm to Abbotshall church
Kirkcaldy	4,500 yards from Abbotshall church to Dysart
Orr Mill	7,500 yards from Dysart to Coaltown near Markinch
Markinch	5,000 yards from Markinch to the summit of the line near New Inn
New Inn	6,000 yards from the summit to Kettle
Collessie	5 miles from Kettle to the summit between there and Lindores
Lindores	5,000 yards from the summit to Clatchet Craig, near Newburgh
Cupar	5 miles from Ladybank to Cupar

As later extensions to the line were approved, further contracts would be let.

During the next two weeks, agreements were completed with the Duke of Buccleuch and John Gladstone over wayleaves on the ferry piers as well as the

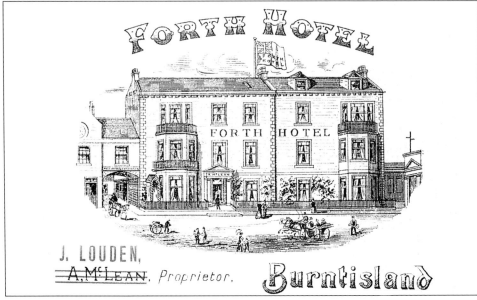

Advertisement for the Forth Hotel, showing a change of proprietors.

Iain Sommerville Collection

Downie's Stables as seen in 1996.   *Author*

use of boats and fares charged. The E&NR took over possession of the ferry for the sum of £90,000 in November 1846 and proudly announced this to a special meeting of shareholders. The transaction included the Burntisland pier, the rights to the crossing, three boats and another one under construction, as well as the Forth Hotel in Burntisland and its adjacent stables and offices. Also covered were the ferry offices at both sides of the Forth.

The Forth Hotel, which was to become an important landmark for visitors to the town, particularly from the ferry, was built in 1823. The original building on the site was the former parish church manse and the Church of Scotland, which built a new manse in Cromwell Road, permitted the extension in 1845. Early tenants of the hotel were the Clarks and the McJanets, but Mrs Horsburgh, who leased the hotel in January 1877, made it the destination in Burntisland for hospitality. It was frequented by the coalmasters of the district when their business in Edinburgh required an early start or a late boat back from Granton and delayed travellers would seek a night's rest there before undertaking the remainder of their journey.

The stables next door were known as Downie's stables after the father and son who ran them, renting gigs or wagonettes to take passengers from the pier or station to Aberdour or other towns to the west. Later occupants of Downie's were Pearson and Jackson, ship chandlers, James Mitchell and Company, shipbrokers and the vice consulates of both Russia and Norway.

The arrangement with Gladstone and the Duke transferred all customs dues leviable on goods both shipped and landed to the company. Harbour dues were negotiated with the burgh council and after much haggling, settled at £1 for each carriage, 10s. for each goods or coal truck and 6s. for each cattle truck landed at Burntisland. In addition, the rights of the port of Kinghorn and Pettycur were transferred to the company for the sum of £4,000. Other incidentals included the right to the free removal of stone from Granton Quarry, and the acceptance of the Duke of Buccleuch that he would be responsible for the laying of rails onto the pier, which the company could use without charge.

James Leslie's plans for the extension of the seaward end of Burntisland pier to take the boats at all tides were approved by the Board. John Grainger was asked to prepare plans for handling goods at Burntisland, since it was proposed that the pier should be for passengers only. Robert Napier was asked to produce two sets of plans, one for a new passenger boat and others to alter existing vessels.

Grainger considered that a short branch to Pettycur pier could be constructed for £500 and this was then included in the first contract. A Bill had later to be sought for the branch and this was presented in January 1846, although work on building the line proceeded without Parliamentary approval. The surveying of the remainder of the line was well underway by the end of August. Rails were offered from the North British's contractor, John Wilson of Dundyvan, at £8 12s. 6d. per ton, estimated at £42,000 for the whole contract, an offer that was not taken up.

The company showed some environmental concern when it sought tenders for bushes and plants for the marginal areas of the line. Two- and three-year-old thorn and beech was sought and half a dozen suppliers from Kirkcaldy and Edinburgh tendered for the contract. The offer of John Reid of Leith was accepted and an order placed for 20,000 thorn bushes at 10s. per thousand and for 50,000 beech at 12s. per thousand.

The initial contract for the Burntisland stretch of the line was given to John Orrell and Company. The first ground was broken at Kinghorn, early in 1846 with the contractor working to the eastern end at Abden and to the west at Burntisland. One of the first accidents occurred at the site of Kinghorn viaduct on 5th June, 1846 when William Galbraith, a superintendent with John Orrell, was killed during the movement of a crane. He was buried in Kinghorn cemetery.

Optimism remained high for, at a special meeting in September, shareholders approved additional branch lines to Leslie, to Leven from either Markinch or Thornton (or both) and then onwards to Anstruther as well as to the Lochgelly coalfield from Kirkcaldy harbour. The plans for this last line were well advanced and shares for it were fully subscribed in a short time. At the end of September, tenders were opened for the first section of the line, Burntisland to Abden, as follows, with the lowest being accepted:

John Barr & Co.	£86,530	Lorimer & Somerville	£79,650
George Milne	£74,595	Kenneth Mathieson Jnr	£72,680
Graham & Sandison	£71,703	Adamson & Fox	£65,100
Robert Dodds	£59,166	Elisha Oldham	£58,796
John Orrell	£57,285		

The managing partners in the successful concern were Mr W. Wightman and Mr William Orrell.

The principal features of the contract were a tunnel and viaduct at Kinghorn, the embankment along the shore to the east of Burntisland Links and the sea wall at Burntisland. Work began on constructing the first section of line at the Bents, near Pettycur. This permitted raw materials to be brought to the site by sea to Pettycur harbour. Orrell employed 8,867 men and 69 horses to start his contract, resulting initially in speedy progress. When the August report was submitted, it showed that almost 140,000 cubic yards of material had been removed in the Burntisland contract, leaving only 120,000 cubic yards to complete.

However, amongst the major contracts, there was some more detailed business for the Board to deal with. In connection with land required for the first contract at Burntisland, James Leven WS was offered around £3,000 for nearly one-third of an acre of garden and some small buildings negotiations for which became lengthy and required resolution in law. Mr James Macfarlane and Miss Macfarlane were offered £1,706 for a dwelling house and garden, whereas Alexander Hutchison received £1,625 for his garden and buildings.

By October, tenders for another two contracts were received, Collessie, north of Ladybank and New Inn at the summit of the route between Markinch and Falkland Road. Many of those who tendered for the first contract tried for later ones, the cost of the Collessie stretch ranging from £19,700 to £16,883, the latter being offered by N. & G. MacDonald. Their tender was accepted but fell on inquiry by the company and a higher tender of £18,261 from W. Kinghorn was sanctioned. This was not an unusual circumstance as railway contracting was a booming business and many tenderers were speculative, unreliable, or even downright dishonest. The New Inn contract was offered to the Dunfermline company of Kenneth Mathieson Jnr at £38,900.

The company considered four tenders for the extension of the branch to Dunfermline in August 1846, those received were:

James Moffat	£34,541
Aitken and Marshall	£32,008
White and Meikle	£26,634
Peter Sinclair	£25,825

However, the Board considered that the contractors were not 'such parties as were likely to carry out the work', and the tender of Walker and Peebles at £36,773 was accepted. The Clunie section was offered to W. Langham for £31,187 and the Lochgelly section was awarded to Anderson and Fox at £39,003. Unfortunately, Walker and Peebles also proved unsuitable and the tender was re-advertised, delaying work further. Kenneth Mathieson was eventually offered the contract for the Dunfermline section at £38,000.

Pettycur Harbour, arrival place of the original Hawthorn locomotives for the E&NR.
James Edmiston Collection

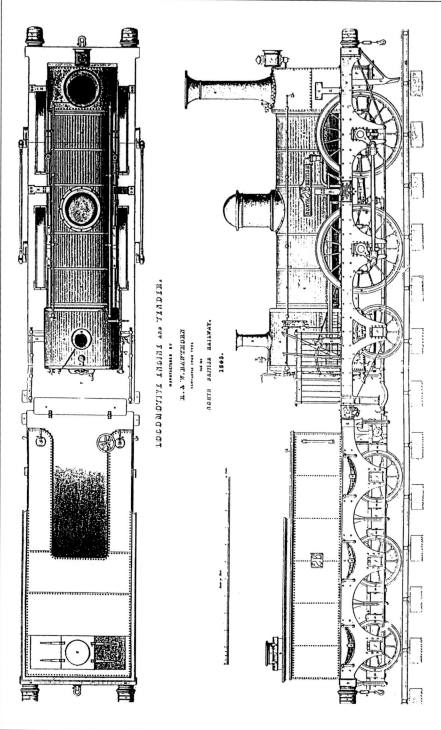

LOCOMOTIVE ENGINE and TENDER.

MANUFACTURED BY

R. & W. HAWTHORN

NEWCASTLE UPON TYNE

FOR THE

NORTH BRITISH RAILWAY.

1846.

Side elevation and plan view for NBR 0-4-2 locomotives from R. & W. Hawthorn in 1845, similar to the design for the Edinburgh and Northern Railway engines.

Author's Collection

Rolling stock

An early decision was made on rolling stock, for Thomas Grainger was requested to contact R. & W. Hawthorn of Newcastle for locomotives and Russell and Macnee of Edinburgh for carriages. A coach making business had been established by Alexander Russell at 4 Princes Street in 1807, and may have joined forces with John Learmonth Junior & Co. in 1837, retaining their name and business address. It appears that Russell may have been the successor to Learmonth senior in the coach building and harness making concern that he ran. The narrow site at Princes Street was unsuitable for coach construction and a yard at Haymarket is likely to have been where the railway coaches were constructed. They vacated the yard in 1851, having sold it to the Edinburgh & Glasgow Railway Company.

John Learmonth, who chaired the sub committee examining rolling stock, retained an interest in many railways in the East of Scotland and in associated industries including his family coach-builders' business. There was even a satirical poem written about him, entitled 'Coachmaker John'. He suggested that the whole order should be for exact duplicates of those ordered for the NBR (of which he was Chairman).

Grainger's enquiries into carriage supply brought details of carriages to be provided by Russell & Macnee 'identical in all respects to those supplied to the North British'. The tender was accepted.

16 First class at £400	£6,400	seating	18 passengers
2 Coupé at £450	£ 900		18 passengers
24 Second class at £225	£5,400		24 passengers
30 Third class at £190	£5,700		36 passengers

Although the number of carriages was quite modest, the complement would allow 1,970 passengers to be conveyed in total at any one time. Couplings for the NBR carriages had been made by James Tod and Sons so it may be assumed that the Edinburgh & Northern Railway contract had couplings from the same source. Tod had shown early interest in the railway through Fife, probably prompted by Learmonth.

Each alternate carriage (except the coupé) was required to be provided with brakes and be delivered with wheels and axles complete. The second class carriages would cost £10 more if plate glass was put into the quarter lights of the otherwise panelled windows, this addition to the specification could be considered before the vehicles were completed. Plate glass was indeed fitted to these carriages which were described as being similar to the first class except for the side cushioning. The third class vehicles were designed to seat 36 passengers on wooden benches around the sides, but provided with only one door per side. The cost of an additional door each side would be an extra £5. To avoid the need to create its own style, the livery of the NBR was adopted, the delivery of the carriages to coincide with the delivery of the locomotives.

The first class carriages were described in a contemporary journal as 'the most modern design, roomy and high roofed'. The third class were reported to be 'comfortable, being covered and lit'. It was the second class that impressed

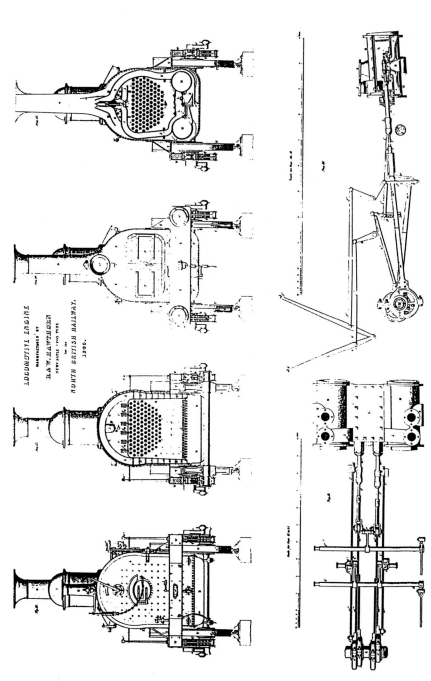

Cross-sections and valvegear for NBR 0-4-2 locomotives from R. & W. Hawthorn in 1845, similar to the design for the Edinburgh and Northern Railway engines.

Author's Collection

the journal most being 'equal to first' in every respect except for the side stuffing. Plate glass was selected by the company for the second class vehicles, as the report comments on this enhancement going on to remark that the doors are the same quality as the first class.

Hawthorn's order for 16 locomotives and tenders was confirmed to the Board on 22nd November, 1845 and valued at £33,805, namely:

3 Light passenger engines at £1,750	£5,250
7 Coupled passenger engines at £1,750	£12,250
6 Heavy goods engines at £1,750	£10,500
The tenders were a separate part of the order, requiring:	
3 at £375 (presumably for the light passenger locomotives)	£1,125
13 at £360	£4,680

The contract required eight of the locomotives to be delivered at Pettycur before May 1847 and the remainder at a rate of one per month thereafter. One quarter of the cost (£8,451 5s.) was payable on 27th April, 1846 and at six-monthly intervals until 27th April, 1847, when further payment would be made on delivery of each engine.

R. & W. Hawthorn was a company closely associated with the development and supply of locomotives in Scotland. The original firm, run by the brothers Robert and William, established the Leith engine works at Great Junction Street during 1846 in order to supply the growing Scottish railways with locomotives. The sea journey from the Forth Banks works in Newcastle was not good for the completed engines and so the parts were made in Newcastle and then sent to Leith for erection. As the orders for other Scottish lines grew, the Leith engine works became responsible for the entire construction of locomotives. With Burntisland only five miles away across the Firth of Forth, it is more than likely that some of the E&NR contract was assembled or even built in Leith.

The goods wagons, like the passenger vehicles, were modest in number and were approved on 23rd December although, unlike the passenger vehicles, not all came from the NBR's suppliers. They were also somewhat cheaper than the NBR ones suggesting that they may not have been quite so substantial in construction:

40 goods vans at £80 10s. from Landale, Kirkcaldy	£3,220
15 horse boxes at £108 16s. from W. McGillivray, Glasgow	£1,632
16 carriage trucks at £79 from T. Barker, Perth	£1,264
10 luggage vans at £83 from J. Henderson & Sons, Kinghorn	£830
The total cost of these orders was	£6,946

Luggage vans were built with open sides and were added to the end of each passenger train. A porter was posted in each van and arranged the luggage for delivery at each successive station on the route. A later development was a composite carriage which Russell and Macnee were asked to consider at the request of the E&NR. Described as having a centre body for 1st class and two outer bodies for 2nd class, the company sought tenders for eight of these new carriages on 9th December, 1846. The first of Russell and Macnee's carriages was due to be delivered by the end of the year and a temporary carriage shed was proposed at Pettycur to accommodate them until required. With one eye on the future, the company required that the structure be able to become permanent once the line was in operation. Ten further

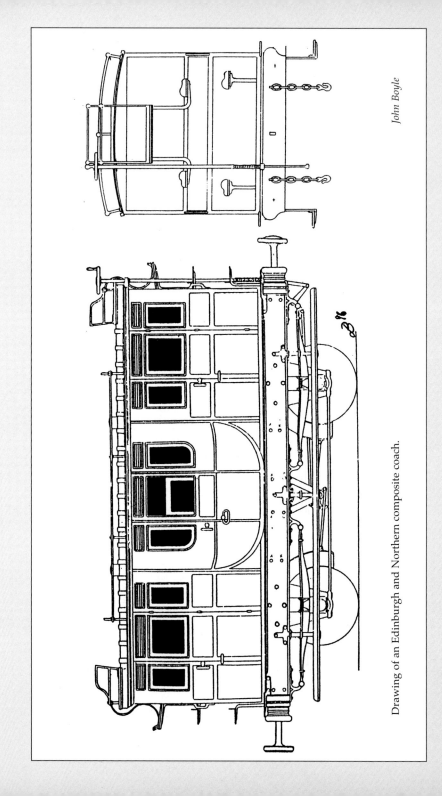

John Boyle

Drawing of an Edinburgh and Northern composite coach.

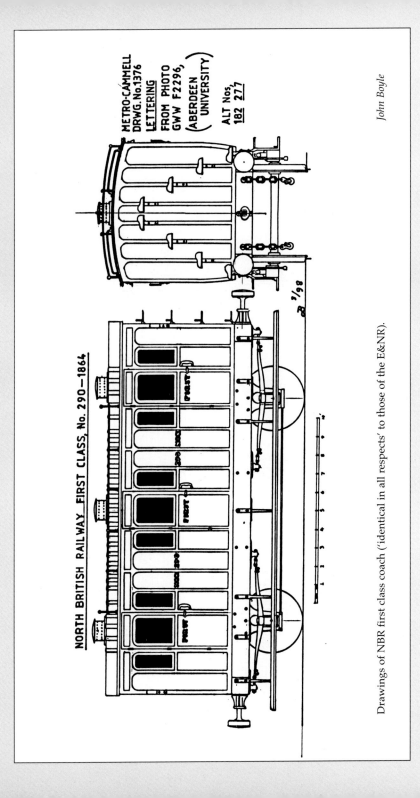

Drawings of NBR first class coach ('identical in all respects' to those of the E&NR).

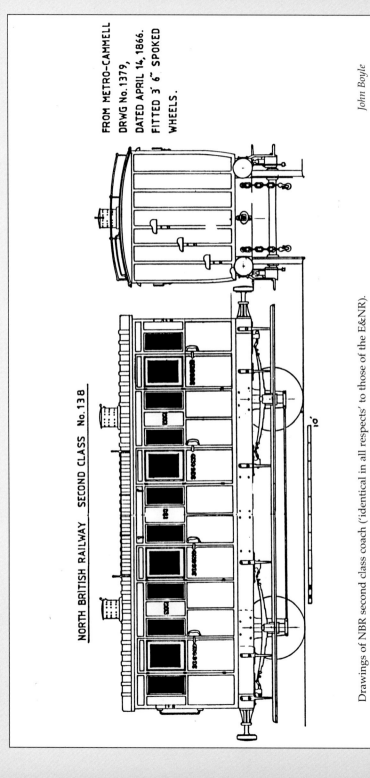

NORTH BRITISH RAILWAY   SECOND CLASS   No. 138

FROM METRO-CAMMELL
DRWG No. 1379,
DATED APRIL 14, 1866.
FITTED 3´ 6˝ SPOKED
WHEELS.

10´

John Boyle

Drawings of NBR second class coach ('identical in all respects' to those of the E&NR).

'stand up' carriages were deemed necessary and contracted for in July 1847. Payment of £720 16s. 5d. was made on 25th October, 1847 to Peter Macpherson for 4th class carriages, so it may be assumed that they were the 10 ordered in July.

One significant omission from these considerations was the need for coal wagons. It was not until November 1846 that the company decided that this essential element of the operation should be ordered. There was no shortage of wagon companies wishing to tender, indeed 27 offers were made for three types of coal wagons including bids from two Dundee businesses, Gourlay, Mudie of Dundee Foundry and Carmichael of Ward Foundry. Prices varied from £77 to £123 per wagon. A later report to the company, shows that payment of £2,548 7s. was made to James Lamb junior of Glasgow in October 1847 for 'coal waggons and Goods train Break carriages' and to Russell and Son of Kirkcaldy for vans (£622 16s.).

The quality of the first three horse boxes supplied by W. McGillivray was considered to be inferior and James Lamb junior and Russell of Kirkcaldy were invited to build six replacements each and the agreement with McGillivray was cancelled.

As demand for transport of livestock grew, the company considered purchasing wagons to satisfy this potential business. Tenders for cattle wagons were presented by:

John Henderson, Kinghorn	£81 each	(sheep wagons, £82)
James Lamb, Glasgow	£91	(for Scotch iron tyres)
	£93	(Bishopwearmouth iron tyres)
	£98	(Bowling Tyres)
James Smith	£84	(sheep wagons £83 17s.)
Alexander Russell, Kirkcaldy	£99	
Payne and Burn	£105	

Henderson was invited to provide six cattle wagons at £81.

Progress slows

The early pace of progress on the line could not be maintained, surveyors and engineers (and reliable contractors) being at a premium during the fast moving years of the Railway Mania. By 26th January, 1846, the Directors were expressing concern that six months had elapsed since the Royal Assent and only three contracts had been let, comprising no more than 12 miles of line. In addition, those works which had been let were progressing very slowly, Tullis observed that many labourers had left to work on the Scottish Central Railway, where wages were better and that there was no urgency apparent among the contractors. Indeed, there was not yet a resident engineer for either the Collessie or New Inn contracts, (resident engineers were to report monthly to Grainger and actually be resident on the contract). The Directors felt that it would be detrimental to the conduct of the railway if the SCR was finished first as it would be able to offer direct connection to Edinburgh by way of Stirling. Capital was also becoming more difficult to raise as the national economy was falling from the peak of Railway Mania and payment of calls for shares was proving to be difficult throughout the country.

At the beginning of February, the London committee was delegated to open negotiations with the proprietors of the Forth ferry to conclude the transfer of the undertaking to the E&NR. On the 19th of the month, Thomas Grainger gave his report on construction progress. The Burntisland section had seen the completion of several bridges and the embankments and walls along the shore. By the end of the month, the sea wall had been built, the viaduct at Kinghorn was complete except for the parapet and wagons were able to cross over. More significantly, the branch line to Pettycur pier was now ready to receive wagons.

The Kinghorn tunnel was also nearing completion with the masonry three-quarters finished. When the tunnel at Kinghorn was under construction, work was begun at either end with the intention of meeting in the middle. However, the bores were not quite as accurate as was expected and they met a few feet apart. Even today, a speed restriction applies through this length of track as trains negotiate the sharper than planned curve where the two halves were re-aligned.

The Invertiel section was ready to commence operations and the line was marked out on the Kirkcaldy section and would be handed over to the contractors in March. The Orr Mill section was not fully marked out and the Markinch contract was let to Ross and Mitchell, the New Inn portion to Kenneth Mathieson and that at Lindores to Kinghorn. The remaining two contracts remained to be let. On the first section, Orrell had fully 8,873 men employed according to reports in June 1847. These were made up of:

794	Masons	5,680 were Scots
170	Joiners	49 were English
140	Smiths	3,144 were Irish
274	Miners	
634	Carters	
6,861	Labourers	

Further compensation was paid to landowners in the Burntisland district as the construction of the line continued. £100 was paid to Burntisland burgh itself for access under the alignment at Scholars Brae, as a bridge was impracticable at that point. Additional land had to be purchased nearby to enable the line to be raised so that an underbridge could be created. It was agreed in February that the pier at Burntisland was inadequate for the purposes of the ferry and the passengers that would use the railway. Thomas Grainger and James Rendell, the civil engineer who had advised on the Tay crossings, were requested to prepare a report on the additional accommodation required and the cost.

Scottish iron masters were keen to share in the expansion of the railways, which the mania had brought, but the local iron industry was not yet fully developed in Scotland and English (or Welsh) companies were often asked to tender for the contracts for rails. The Edinburgh & Northern Railway Company obtained rail from North East England, sea conveyance of which was the most efficient. The Middlesborough firm of Bolckow and Vaughan, and Morrissey, Jansen and Company of Newcastle were both asked to supply the E&NR. It would be reasonable to assume that Pettycur was the port to which the rail was transported since this was the port for the delivery of the locomotives. One Scottish company, the East of Scotland Malleable Iron Company, did also provide rails although its existence was short-lived. Tenders for sleepers were also sought. They were required to be larch, Scots fir, Baltic fir or red pine and either triangular or semi-circular in profile. Offer prices varied from 2s. 3d. to 4s. 6d. although the highest price was considered to be expensive.

A supply of pure water was also sought to supply the works and the locomotives. Grainger was asked to arrange for pipes to be laid from Grange Hill above Kinghorn to the Links. Ten water cranes in all were supplied by Alexander Russell of Kirkcaldy for the line, while at Ladybank, a 6 hp engine was purchased from Kinmond, Hutton and Steel to raise a supply from a well to be dug there.

The Roundhouse

The company had created a particularly strong position for itself by promising to create the locomotive workshops at the town with the additional employment that would be provided. Grainger believed that the ground at the Lammerlaws in Burntisland for the proposed works might be too small and that an adjacent piece of the Links on the east side would be more suitable. As we have seen, the town council of Burntisland had not been particularly co-operative with railway companies that wished to bring trade to its burgh, mainly because of the damage that would be created in the cramped High Street area near the harbour. Now it was the Links that had to be protected. The Links was (and is) a piece of open land between the main streets and the shore given to the people of the town by King James V and used for public recreation.

On 10th July, 1845, a sub-committee of the E&NR considered an agreement, which had been sent to the company by the town clerk of Burntisland, to make use of some of this open space. The Secretary was instructed to correspond with the Provost of the burgh over the removal from the agreement of a clause protecting the company from objections made by 'parties interested in the road' through the Links. Although there were clear benefits in having improved road access, the E&NR was reluctant to lose hard won advantages from the council and attempted to overcome the dissension that resulted. Inevitably, legal battles ensued and an interdict was taken out at the High Court in Edinburgh to prevent the company taking possession of the land. By November 1846, the burgh had agreed to transfer the land to the company, but with restrictions on the height of any building erected on the north side of the land.

The works occupied the triangular parcel of land to the north of Lammerlaws bridge and to the east of the railway. Considering the line was created in the early years of railways, the building was impressive. The solid stone roundhouse was 145 feet in diameter and 22 feet high with walls which were three feet thick. Surmounted by a conical roof, whose peak reached 75 feet high, it was an imposing building for its time. This was supported by 54 round iron trusses in addition to cross- and under-bindings. The roof was protected with slate. The central turntable was a modest 45 ft in diameter, but more than adequate for the locomotives which had been ordered from R. & W. Hawthorn, and in turn gave access to 14 internal roads. Those which were not through roads had inspection pits, but three led to the erecting shop, the lathe shop and a head shunt.

Burntisland Roundhouse in early LNER days.   *Author's Collection*

Burntisland Roundhouse in the 1930s with roof vents removed.   *Bill Lynn Collection*

The building was part of an extended works complex and doubled both as a locomotive depot and workshop for light repairs, the whole site being known to the locals as 'The Roundhouse'. The adjacent erecting shop saw the manufacture of engines although some fabrication of components was undertaken in the roundhouse. Repairs were also undertaken on the fleet of ferryboats, which made the crossing to Granton. These were more frequent than expected for the crews had the strange habit of using water straight from the Forth in the boilers, resulting in damage to the internal workings of the boats.

The appointment of a locomotive superintendent was also an important one for the company and the position was offered in September 1846 to Robert Nicholson, who was the superintendent of locomotives at Berwick station on the North British Railway. His name was put forward to the Board by Robert Hawthorn and he was offered a yearly salary of £170 until the line was opened, after which time it would be reviewed. It was suggested that he begin his employment within three weeks, on the Edinburgh, Leith and Granton line, although he immediately set about reviewing the requirements of the main line both in equipment and motive power. The first of his staff was not appointed until July 1847, when Edward Sproat was named as his assistant for the Edinburgh and Granton section of the line.

By October 1846, the Board was considering the shipment of locomotives from Hawthorn and asked for an earlier delivery. Hawthorn agreed to 1st April, 1847 and the consignment of two per month thereafter. Nicholson began to doubt whether the motive power order was sufficient for his needs and asked the E&NR Board to consider extra locomotives. The Directors approved an additional ten. Plans for the works had not yet been submitted for approval and Grainger was pressed to prepare them as soon as possible, no doubt urged on by Robert Nicholson.

The locomotive depot at Ladybank was placed under the charge of another assistant, Thomas Waddell, who had previously been an engineman on the NBR line. Ladybank also became the headquarters of the civil engineer's department. The appointment of a foreman at Burntisland (who would also assist Nicholson) was agreed; a second assistant being the foreman of the wrights and the coachbuilders who was paid £100 per annum. James Ellis was appointed the wagon shop foreman in 1848. (Later, his grandson, John Allan, also a railwayman, would become Provost of Dunfermline and write a series of articles in the *Dunfermline Press* about his family and railway reminiscences.) The foremen were paid an annual salary in line with the other senior employees of £120. A storekeeper was also appointed. John Bissett, who came from Arncroach, near St Monans, was paid £60 per annum. Additionally there were eight enginemen and eight firemen based at Burntisland, among them John Elder, James Macpherson, Allan Gibson, Robert Cochrane and John Horne. One engineman, Peter Isles, was enticed from the Dundee & Arbroath Railway and gave the company honourable service, being the last Burntisland driver to cross the original Tay Bridge.

The relationship between the railway workshops and the ferries was a close one and the superintendent of ferries would work closely with the locomotive superintendent. Captain Field was offered the former position at a salary of £2 per week in April 1847. The wages of the seamen were increased from 14s. to 16s. per week at the same time.

In 1848, a shipwright and a boilersmith were employed to handle the work needed on the ferries. In order to make the most of their skills, it was agreed

PS *Auld Reekie* in the outer harbour at Burntisland, Rossend Castle in the background. The condition of the outer harbour is apparent.
Kirkcaldy Museum/240.3

between Nicholson and Captain Field that these two men would be available to the locomotive department when not employed on shipping. An illustration of the range of responsibilities in such a new enterprise came when Nicholson submitted a sketch to the locomotive committee in January 1849, for a fire engine to be established at Burntisland.

Prior to the completion of the line from Burntisland, a further Act came into force, transferring the rights of the Granton to Burntisland ferry to the Edinburgh & Northern Railway Company. It became necessary, therefore, for the company to purchase goods boats to run in addition to the two passenger ferries which were, at that time, plying the crossing. The boats, which the E&NR inherited were PS *Edinburgh Castle* and PS *Thane of Fife*, both over 25 years old by that time. Neither was used by the company. John Gladstone retained his own boat, PS *Maid of Leven* until January 1847 when he then chartered it to the company which in turn transferred it to the Tay crossing.

Two new passenger vessels were ordered by the E&NR from Miller and Ravenhill at Blackwall. A new PS *Thane of Fife* and PS *Auld Reekie* were promised to be available on the Forth by November 1847, but were late due to modifications which were required to be made to them to suit the slipways at Granton and Burntisland. Captain Field submitted a report on the alterations required to be made to PS *Auld Reekie*. In his account to the Board on 19th January, 1848 he reported that all work would be completed before the arrival of the boats at Burntisland so that nothing more need be done by the company.

The first two locomotives were not delivered from Hawthorn's until August 1848, followed later in the month by three more. Delivery of the engines is believed to have been made to Pettycur pier, where rails had been laid down from the main line, rather than at Burntisland itself, where the pier did not have direct rail provision at first. The sequence of delivery of E&NR engines is difficult to deduce owing to the two centres used by Hawthorn's but, using various sources, a possible pattern appears in Appendix One.

The Line Opens

The Board of Trade inspection of the line was carried out on 3rd September, 1847 and the inspector declared himself highly satisfied with 'the substantial and really scientific manner in which the whole of the contractors had executed their proportion of the work'. As a consequence of the completion of the contract, Orrell laid off 7,331 men, of whom 4,809 were Scots, 2,511 were Irish and 11 were English. In addition, 70 prime horses were sold off. Preparations to begin public services were already advanced and invitations to the formal opening were instructed on 8th September.

The ceremony to open the line was held at Cupar on 17th September, 1847, by which time, John Balfour had succeeded Learmonth as Chairman. The first two trains set out from there and met 'a very large company' who had crossed from Edinburgh to Burntisland. At Markinch, exuberant sightseers had forced an entry on to some of the 20 coaches in the leading train, but most were immediately ejected. However, some were inadvertently taken onwards to Burntisland, where the wrongdoers were thrown off the train and left to make their own way back! At Burntisland, the guests from Edinburgh, then boarded the special trains, the leading one under the command of Thomas Grainger, the Engineer of the line, and returned to Cupar just after twelve noon.

The journey was slow because of the crowds that lined the route, taking almost an hour and a half to return to Cupar. There the traditional collation was served in a spacious pavilion to between 600 and 700 people along with 'unlimited champagne'. The journey through Fife was accompanied by what must have seemed like the entire population of the Kingdom lining the route, waving and cheering as the two trains passed. The returning parties left Cupar, for a second time, in two trains, the first departed at 4.00 pm travelling more speedily than before, running non-stop to connect with the evening ferry to Edinburgh.

The first regular passenger trains ran on 20th September departing at 7.00 am from both Edinburgh and Cupar. The initial timetable saw further departures at 10.30 am and 1.40 pm and 4.40 pm from Edinburgh and at 10.00 am, 2.00 pm and 4.00 pm from Cupar. Patronage on the first day was much greater than had been expected putting considerable pressure on the coach service between Cupar and Dundee. By the end of the month, additional trains were required from Dysart to meet the 8.15 am ferry to Granton and two others from Edinburgh to Lindores. The time allowed between Edinburgh and the departure from Burntisland was 55 minutes.

Plans for the locomotive works engine house and carriage sheds were initially requested in October 1846, the land for the roundhouse being available and staked out by February 1847. The contract was given to MacDonald, who had tendered to construct sections of the line. By July 1848, MacDonald had reported that steps had been taken to acquire the ground for the Roundhouse. Nicholson was not, however, prepared to wait for the permanent structure and he set up temporary shops until the works became available. He set about equipping them with bellows and anvils from Russell of Kirkcaldy. Tools, lathes and other equipment costing a total of £2,600 was purchased in April 1847.

Power supply for the new workshops was sought and Russell of Kirkcaldy, R. & W. Hawthorn and Kinmond, Hutton and Steel of Dundee all offered tenders for either a beam or horizontal engine. Nicholson preferred the horizontal engine and asked if Russell could supply one for the price, which Hawthorn offered at £670. The Russell engine was chosen and proved to be a good choice, performing sterling service at the works and powering the machinery until wagon repairs ceased under BR in the 1960s. Even then, it remained in use as wagon repairs continued throughout LNER days. There were only four men in charge of this engine during its life, Tom Slimmings, John Turpie, James Spiers and James Napier.

However, capital was tight in 1847 and tenders for the construction of the locomotive works were not sought until March 1849. By then the responsibility was given to the company's newly appointed Manager, who, at the beginning of 1850, was asked to provide an estimate for the construction of a carriage shed, 'to be done as cheaply as possible'. The whole enterprise was not complete and ready for business until 1851. However, the carriage sheds were tendered for in March

1847 by two of those who tendered for the station contract. Bonthrone and Robertson offered to erect the shed for £1,113 and Francis Farquharson for £1,240. The latter's tender was accepted as it included the necessary rock cutting.

Burntisland was not the largest of towns and the increase in population that would result from an influx of staff for the line would put pressure on existing housing. Plans for homes for the employees of the line were requested by the Board in July 1847. The town was also to benefit from the provision of telegraph communication and the Electric Telegraph Company was authorised to erect poles along the route of both the E&NR and the Granton line.

The Directors became concerned that Robert Nicholson was concentrating on major repairs of some of the engines and not on the day to day responsibilities of his department. With an eye to the financial implications, they did not wish that the work being done became so substantial that it should properly be charged to capital account. They issued an instruction in January 1850, before completion of the building, that no work, which could be charged to the company's capital account, was to be carried out at the 'locomotive institution of the Company'. Any such work was to be done by outside contractors. In March, the minutes recorded: 'In order to more effectively ensure the undivided attention of the locomotive superintendent to the working of the line, the extension of all works (except the incidental repair and maintenance of rolling stock) has been discontinued at Burntisland and will be contracted for'. This instruction would suggest that new building of engines should not be carried out at Burntisland. However, some new building was later carried out, but mostly repairs and rebuilding was undertaken.

The adequacy of the Burntisland works in the early years has always been in question, for arrangements were made for some of the repairs to locomotives to be carried out at the Perth works of the Scottish Central Railway. This may also have been because of the poor condition of some of the locomotives, due both to the lack of regular maintenance and heavy driving as well as to the backlog of work at Burntisland which resulted.

Evidence for this came as early as 1848, when a passenger, Sir William Dunbar, accused drivers of driving recklessly and Nicholson was asked to discipline them. The locomotive superintendent also agreed that the engines were not well kept, being in constant use, with little time even to clean them. The exposure to the weather contributed, especially at Perth where there was no shed to keep them in. At the outset of 1854, the Edinburgh, Perth and Dundee Railway (as the Edinburgh & Northern had now become, *see next chapter*) recorded 42 locomotives in use, of which 19 were passenger engines and 14 were goods based at Burntisland. Nine further were in use on the Granton section. In the summer of 1854, Nicholson reported that there were eight engines under repair at Burntisland. Five needed heavy repairs and three only light work.

Indeed, so poor was the condition of one 0-6-0 locomotive, No. 35, built by Hawthorn's, that Alexander Allan, locomotive superintendent of the SCR, refused to effect any repairs on it when it was received at Perth in March 1857. He had the pieces placed on a truck and returned them to Burntisland. The locomotive was less than one year old.

Rolling stock in January 1854 comprised 204 passenger vehicles and 1,574 goods vehicles:

Burntisland station building on 22nd June, 1889. Cranes in the background work on the line to the Forth Bridge while an unidentified NB 4-4-0 sits in the passenger shed.   *Bill Roberton*

The 1847 station buildings with coaches stored in the platform lines, 1961.

James F. McEwan/N3312

34 1st class	20 composites	29 2nd class	60 3rd class
17 4th class	20 horse boxes	16 carriage trucks	8 train breaks [sic]
68 cattle	60 vans	262 flat wagons	
17 break vans	1,147 coal wagons	20 coke wagons	

Perhaps the growth in Mr Young's cattle exporting business explains the large number of cattle wagons on the company's books.

Stations

Plans for both Burntisland and Kirkcaldy stations were first requested in July 1846, the Directors reserving the right to inspect and determine the position of those and several other stations. On a visit to the Burntisland site, the Directors agreed that there should be easy access from the station to both sides of the pier. The space on the east was appropriate for passengers (being on the leeward side) and the west was considered suitable for goods although more land would need to be acquired. A loading bank could be constructed if the extra land could stretch to the high water mark. Mr Hutchison's land should be obtained and raised to the level of the station, and spoil could provide the land to the west of the pier. The old coal shed at the top of the pier should be removed. The Board also examined the land in front of the Forth Hotel, concluding that any ornamentation there would be wasted as it lay in the way of the entrance to the station.

The ferry pier at Burntisland lay to the east of the harbour entrance and ran out into the Forth at right angles to the shore, immediately adjacent to the station building. The pier was completely exposed to the unpredictable river and, as the pierhead faced Forth Place, little protection was afforded. Once services had commenced, passengers had only a short walk from the pier to the station and the relative comfort of Messrs Russell and Macnee's carriages, but in inclement weather, this brief journey could be unpleasant. Shelter for passengers soon became the subject of comment from passengers including local gentry in the person of Lord Leven and the pier therefore became the subject of further serious consideration by the company. Grainger was instructed to report on a solution. The intention was to ensure the division of passengers and goods either through different piers or separate use of each side of the existing one.

Further sites were selected for stations along the line, that at Kirkcaldy being 'best behind Balsusney House' the house itself would be considered as a hotel. At Kinghorn, the station was to be at the west end of the town where originally planned, a house facing the street would be acquired by the company and suffice as an entrance. By the end of August, more serious consideration was being given to the additional land at Burntisland pier, but this was later deferred until the customs and shore dues were settled.

During the autumn, there was consternation among the Board at the delay in furnishing plans for the station at Burntisland, frequent requests having been made to Grainger as early as October 1846. Throughout the autumn, plans were repeatedly sought, the tenders for the construction of the station building not

Platform side of Burntisland 1847 building, showing outline of canopies, in 1996.

Author

Remains of 1847 platform buildings at Burntisland (former railway social club) in 1996.

Author

being considered until 17th February, 1847, and even then consideration was delayed. The tender offered were:

D. Norman	£3,920	F. Farquharson	£4,000
Bonthrone & Robertson	£4,180	W. Thomson	£4,190
James Mill	£4,267	John Turnbull	£4,423

The lowest of £3,920 was from D. Norman but this was subject to a degree of uncertainty and the contract was eventually awarded to Francis Farquharson of Farquharson and Durward.

The station building, now a listed structure which still stands alongside the harbour, was built in stone with an imposing frontage welcoming passengers from a stormy ferry crossing with a reassuringly solid appearance. The two-storey building, attributed to Perth architect Andrew Heiton, has an arcaded frontage at the ground floor entrance, which faces west, and a Georgian three-bay upper storey that housed the offices. Behind this was a train shed with a double pitched canopy over the three, the original iron roof being provided by Messrs Robertson and Lister for the sum of £595, although this has long since been demolished. Kinghorn station seems to have been a more straightforward affair. Agreement was reached between Henry Lees and Kinghorn town council as early as 11th March, 1845, and formalised a year later.

The complement of railway servants at Burntisland was about a quarter of the total employed on the line. The station superintendent, Alexander Macdonald, was the most senior official at Burntisland and he was paid the sum of £120 per annum. Among his staff was his son who was the first class booking clerk, paid 27s. per week and John Paton junior, the second and third class booking clerk, also paid 27s. per week. The four first class guards, each paid 24s., were James Young, William Elder, Thomas Swan and C. Fairfoul. The four second class guards, paid 22s., were D. Wallace, T. Kay, George Pillans and I. Fraser. Other known wages at the time were: First porter 18s. per week, 7 porters 16s. per week, pointsman 22s. per week

John Arthur was appointed as the sub-goods manager, responsible to the goods manager, Charles McGlashan based in Edinburgh, and he received an annual salary of £120. McGlashan whose address was given as 21 Norton Place, Edinburgh, was paid £250 annually and began his duties on the Edinburgh, Leith & Granton Railway. John Arthur came highly recommended by Mr Swan and other influential gentlemen in Kirkcaldy. Other positions included, two goods porters, Henry King and Alexander Cameron, 18s. and two junior goods porters, one of whom was named David Balfour, 16s., one goods clerk, Robert McGregor, 23s. per week and one goods weigher, Thomas Shephard, 18s. per week.

On the ferry service, a pier master was needed both at Burntisland and Granton. Recommended by Mr Cameron, a former stagecoach guard called Brand who had worked on Alexander McNab's Fife coaches was appointed to Burntisland as pier foreman and James Buchanan was appointed to Granton.

The line's first accident was fortunately none too severe, resulting in the derailment of some carriages on a train passing through the rock cutting near Lammerlaws on 1st October, 1847. It was caused by stones being scattered across the line from the workings of Farquharson and Durward the contractors for the station building at Burntisland. The foreman, James Swan, was deemed to be at fault and was discharged.

In April 1848, the Board of the Edinburgh & Northern Railway, prompted by Landale, one of the Directors, acknowledged the work that Alexander McNab had done to develop the coach traffic between the Forth and the Tay. As a token (literally) of its gratitude, the Board presented McNab with a free ticket for the line, in the form of disc engraved on both sides. McNab had operated the coaches from Cupar and had been a great supporter of the line. The face of the token showed a locomotive with the company's name and the year. The reverse was engraved:

To
Alexander Macnab Esq
Cupar, Fife.
This free ticket
To travel on the Railway is
Presented by the Directors
In acknowledgement of
His public spirited exertions
For the improvement of the
Means of communication
Through Fifeshire
April 1848
Henry Lees Secy

Progress at the northern end of the route saw the E&NR reach Perth on 18th July, 1848, courtesy of the Strathearn Railway, a company set up specifically to deal with the Scottish Central's stance on the shared line through Moncrieff tunnel into Perth. The branch to Newport was completed along with the crossing to Broughty Ferry.

The Dunfermline branch line opened from Thornton to Crossgates in September 1848. Trains made connection at Thornton with services from either Burntisland or Ladybank and passengers were taken onwards from Crossgates by coach. Stations were opened near Bowhill and at Lochgelly and Cowdenbeath, where there was also a coach connection from Kinross. The E&NR named the Bowhill station 'Cardenden', although a settlement of that name did not exist before this time. The branch was not initially appealing to passengers travelling from Edinburgh since the coach road to the Queensferry was simpler and more straightforward.

At a meeting of shareholders on 15th March, 1848, the Board had announced that it was buying shares in the Stirling & Dunfermline Railway Company (S&DR). The S&DR was wooed by both the Scottish Central Railway and the Edinburgh & Glasgow Railway, companies which would have been able to filter the West Fife coal traffic towards the West of Scotland. The Edinburgh & Northern Railway was determined to protect its hard won traffic from West Fife.

Time consistency was always a problem for early railways as clocks were set by the sun, and not by a central source. Greenwich Mean Time was adopted in Edinburgh on 29th January, 1848 and so this time was substituted for local time on all the company's timetables.

Chapter Three

The Edinburgh, Perth & Dundee Railway

On 7th August, 1847, the Edinburgh, Leith & Granton Railway placed its operations under the control of the Edinburgh & Northern Railway, prior to the opening of the latter railway. The joint company initially took the name of the E&NR following the Royal Assent for the Act (11 Vict. cap. ccxxxix) on 22nd July. Following the purchase of the EL&GR, the company became known as the Edinburgh, Perth & Dundee Railway (EP&DR). John Balfour was appointed Chairman, with James Burnett as Vice Chairman.

Thomas Bouch, Manager

It was on 13th January, 1849 that John Balfour announced the name of a comparative unknown who was about to join the E&NR as Manager, although he described him as 'a gentleman of great experience in the working and development of railway traffic'. Bouch came with a grand sense of vision and yet he would later be associated with the greatest of all Victorian railway disasters. He believed that construction costs of new lines could be reduced and encouraged the growth of new branch lines with what became known, most appropriately, as the cheap railway movement. His vision was of slender viaducts and he could see that the two firths, Forth and Tay, had to be crossed by rail sooner rather than later. His brother, William, was the locomotive superintendent of the Stockton & Darlington Railway and he had resigned as resident engineer on that line to come to Scotland.

Thomas Bouch was born in Thursby, Cumberland in 1822 and after an undistinguished career in the North of England, came from the Stockton & Darlington to Burntisland. Although the construction of the great bridges was some decades away, Bouch was shortly to be responsible for the design and introduction of an ingenious method of transportation across both the Forth and the Tay, the world's first roll-on, roll-off ferry.

Bouch's arrival at the E&NR was inauspicious for another reason. The company had not prepared accommodation for him and on his first day, had to find a spare room at the company's offices in Edinburgh. At his first Board meeting on 20th January, he announced that he had sacked four members of staff for various misdemeanours. This was to form the tone of his early weeks in the post of manager for he promptly dismissed nine cleaners, five joiners, a smith, a striker and a wagon greaser on his visit to the works at Burntisland two weeks later. Bouch assumed the role of engineer on the line and took responsibility for the pier staff at Burntisland, Granton, Tayport and Broughty Ferry.

There was an extraordinary meeting of shareholders in the popular Gibb's Royal Hotel, Edinburgh on Tuesday, 30th January, 1849 to discuss the financial structure of the new company prior to re-incorporation. John Balfour, Chairman, recapped on the finances from the outset and the plans for the future. The share capital on the E&NR was £1,363,260 prior to 1848 with loans of £454,418. The neighbouring Edinburgh, Leith & Granton Railway was incorporated with share capital of £320,677 and loans of £137,267 giving a combined total of £2,276,622. He went on to outline the expenditure, which totalled £2,232,115. This included £1,020,504 for the E&NR plus similar amounts for the two extensions, £246,617 for the Newport line and £264,423 for the Dunfermline branch. Correspondingly, the ferries had close on the same amounts expended on them, £67,082 at Burntisland and £54,688 on the Tay Ferry. The line cost £33,000 per mile to construct although the Fife lines had cost only £25,000 per mile. The company reckoned that it needed a further £72,885 to complete its plans.

The Engineer's estimate for construction of the route had been exceeded by 16 per cent, the primary explanation being that the original line was planned to have been single but during the Parliamentary process, double track was ordered. Later works exceeded estimate by only 8 per cent. This was common in the early days of railway construction as was another reason, that of higher compensation. Landowners along the line had generally been agreeable to the line being built but when it came to money, they put up greater resistance until compensation was extracted. In addition, there were the legal costs to defend themselves against predatory lines, (the Edinburgh & Perth Railway in particular) and difficult neighbours like the Scottish Central Railway and its intractability at Moncrieffe tunnel which had been much greater than anticipated.

However, John Balfour struck a positive note in briefly announcing that receipts over the previous six months had averaged £2,000 per week coming mainly from passenger traffic. As goods and mineral traffic improved, revenue was expected to double. Once the 3½ mile completion of the Dunfermline branch was executed, annual revenues were expected to be good.

Passengers	£105,300
Goods	£56,160
Minerals	£79,300
Total	£240,760

With expenses running at 45 per cent of receipts (£108,342), the annual net revenue was expected to be £132,418.

In April 1849, the Edinburgh & Northern Railway was re-incorporated as the Edinburgh, Perth & Dundee Railway under an Act (13 Vict. cap. lxxix). The main aim of this Act was to restructure the company financially; the change of name now more closely reflected the three points of the 'y' shaped route through Fife which the line described. An additional £310,000 was authorised under the Act. The locomotives of the EL&GR were not incorporated into the stock lists of the EP&DR until all the payments had been made, sometime in 1855.

Operational Obstacles

As the new company settled down to its day to day operation, there were a number of complaints about the train service and the ticket arrangements. One complaint in July 1849 was that, from Burntisland, there were no evening trains with the required parliamentary coaches offering cheap travel at one penny per mile. In February, 1850, following a complaint from a passenger, Mr Spink, return fares to Edinburgh from stations in Fife were introduced but only on two days per week, Wednesday and Saturday.

	1st class	2nd class	3rd class
From Kirkcaldy and Sinclairtown,	3s. 6d.	2s. 6d.	1s. 6d.
From Dysart	3s. 6d.	2s. 9d.	1s. 8d.
Burntisland had return fares daily	2s. 6d.	2s. 3d.	

Weekly tickets were abolished at the same time, these had been set at 5s. in 1848 to encourage trade, but now seemed to be over-generous.

Another complaint came from a shareholder, Mr Cockshott. He had found it unpleasant to share the facilities at Burntisland station with cattle which were being carried across the Forth. Agreement was reached that this was not acceptable and that cattle should be kept outside the station yard and that a piece of land should be sought to provide for this.

The company blamed incorrect timetables on Thomas Bouch when Messrs Blacklock and Bradshaw complained in September 1850 that the company had not sent revisions to them for two months. The monthly *Bradshaws* were to become legendary and their reputation was at stake if each company did not submit a regular monthly report. The Manager was asked to look in to the matter and ensure that it did not recur. The *Fife Herald* commented in October 1850 that many of the third class carriages remained unlit with the lamps devoid of oil.

Perhaps the complaint that revealed most about the way the railway was being run took the form of a letter to the *Fifeshire Journal* on Thursday 21st August, 1851. It provides a graphic illustration of the practices, which the railways permitted in the early years.

Sir, Permit me thro' your columns to draw attention of Railway Directors to a most dangerous and reprehensible practice now followed by the guards on our local railway. On certain trains, leaving the Kirkcaldy Station, the guards are in the habit of checking the passenger's tickets by passing from carriage to carriage and that while the train is at full speed. Think of these poor men walking along a few inches of board, grasping at handrails and leaning in at carriage doors with the train going at a rate of some twenty to thirty miles an hour! The thing is insanity and I wonder why some of them have not been crushed to atoms long ere now. There is surely no necessity for the practice. Better lose a few minutes at Kinghorn than endanger valuable lives; or if lives are not cared for, I feel confident there is no passenger of sense who would not willingly forego a few minutes of time rather than his or her feelings harrowed by the fear of every moment hearing the death shriek of some of these poor men beneath the wheels of the impetuous train. I call upon the Directors to put a stop to the practice and should they not, I will certainly take means to have it brought before the share holders at the next general meeting.

Although the concept of newspaper kiosks was not well developed at the time, nevertheless, there was a request to the company by Alexander Murray to sell newspapers on board trains and ferries. He made a proposal of £35 per annum for the rights an offer that was accepted by the Board on 11th June, 1850, on the condition that the sum was paid in advance or security found.

Notable travellers to the towns of Fife attracted the attention of the press. One such passenger on the Edinburgh, Perth & Dundee Railway was the author of

Edinburgh, Perth & Dundee Railway

First saloon and second compartment coach, built 1858-1859 at Burntisland
Length over headstocks - 20 ft
Width overall - 8 ft 0 in.
Wheels - 3 ft diameter

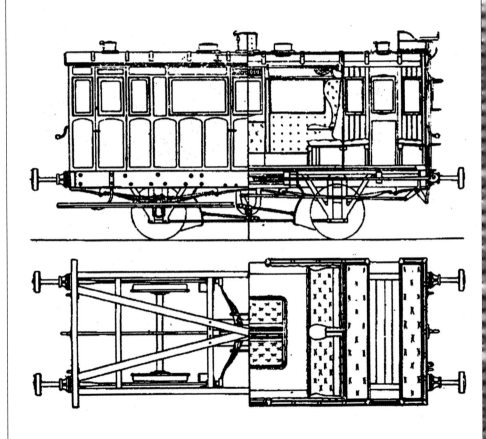

John Boyle Collection

Uncle Tom's Cabin, Harriet Beecher Stowe, who was travelling from Dundee to Edinburgh on a lecture tour. Her journey was noted in the *Fifeshire Advertiser*. She, her professor husband and brother arrived two hours late at Burntisland station on 30th April, 1853, and crossed on the 4.10 pm ferry to Granton. Almost apologetically, the newspaper reported that as it was not known that she was coming, there were few people out to greet her, although after her delayed journey she looked 'somewhat care-worn'. The party (apparently) still reached Edinburgh in good time and Harriet Beecher Stowe was able to give her lecture.

In July 1850, the company, along with the Duke of Buccleuch and Queensberry and Sir John Gladstone, was granted an interdict (or injunction) against Andrew Greig, the lessee of the ferry from Granton to Burntisland. Greig, of Chain Pier Inn at Trinity, had contravened his lease by planning a private pleasure cruise in his boat, PS *Rob Roy*, from the pier at Burntisland. Pleasure cruises on the Forth were a popular outing for the people of Edinburgh, Burntisland becoming the destination for excursions. In addition, in July 1850, 'a large pleasure party' from the Edinburgh Total Abstinence Society travelled to Dunfermline, via Thornton and Burntisland, the first group to make the trip since the branch had opened.

The company's coaches were suffering wear and tear after two years working along the line. At the end of April, Russell and Macnee tendered to paint the carriages at a cost of £22 each for first class and £18 for a second class. The company's coat of arms could be applied at £1 10s. extra. It is worthy of note that the company's minutes do not refer to 'repaint', leaving speculation that they had been delivered in a somewhat basic condition. However, cautious not to spend money recklessly, the traffic committee did not sanction this expenditure insisting that the work be done at either Heriot Hill or Burntisland and done as cheaply as possible by the staff. In April, the traffic committee also considered a reduction on the cost of the locomotive department, inviting both Nicholson and the newly appointed Bouch to examine expenditure.

Some of the company's road vehicles were not worthy of repair and the following advertisement appeared in the *Fifeshire Advertiser* on 19th January, 1856:

For Sale, Six Common Road Four-Wheeled Covered or Box Vans each 9ft long and 5 ft wide mounted on springs. Wheels three feet and four feet Diameter. Each van is fitted with screw brake and shafts for one horse. Apply to Robt Nicholson, locomotive superintendent.

Uniforms, like the coaches, began to show signs of wear and tenders were invited for replacements. Two tenders were submitted for guard's uniforms. John Clapperton and Company proposed £3 19s. 3d. per suit excluding embroidery, but allowing for an oiled silk cover to the cap. Marshall and Aitken offered to supply the same outfit (without silk cover) for £3 8s. 2d., an offer which was accepted. A porter named McDonald, who was based at Burntisland, wrote to the traffic committee in January 1849 requesting the replacement of his uniform, to which the committee agreed providing that it was over one year old.

As goods manager, Charles McGlashan must have held an important place in the development of trade in the East of Scotland at this time. In order to obtain advantageous rates for the transport of their merchandise, traders needed to be favoured by McGlashan. Whether in gratitude for a predisposed attitude towards them, or perhaps in order to secure it, it is not clear but an act of near bribery took place in May 1849. McGlashan was entertained to dinner by his customers and presented with an elegant tea and coffee service, an event, which even merited an announcement in the *Fifeshire Advertiser* on the 19th May.

Although a longer route, the Scottish Central Railway's line via Perth, Stirling and the E&GR was considered more attractive to both passengers and freight alike, because there was no change of carriage, a point intensely promoted by the SCR. There were also minor battles over fares for the two routes, which simply confirmed the uncompetitive nature of the ferry crossings and the vulnerability of the EP&DR to its rivals.

Bouch's Floating Railway

On his arrival in Scotland, Thomas Bouch had set about planning on how the Edinburgh, Perth & Dundee Railway could overcome the drawbacks of the two major ferry crossings. Twice on their northern journey from Edinburgh, passengers or goods would have to be transferred from train to a ferry and twice they would have to be loaded back onto another train before completing the trip. This was expensive in both time and labour, with the operating costs of the ferries being six times that of operating the railway. Such expense put the company at a disadvantage over its competitors. A further obstacle was the inability of the railway to handle large cargoes, as cranes at the quaysides were ineffective for the increasing loads carried.

As early as July 1847, Grainger had been asked by the Board to seek ways of 'slipping goods at Burntisland and Granton without unloading the trucks'. Despite the lack of a solution, the company had not given up on the idea. Grainger had proposed hydraulic cranes to lift wagons on board the boats, singly in cradles, and recommended Armstrong of Newcastle to supply them and they were subsequently ordered. Two cranes with engines and machinery were actually made and ready for installation at Burntisland before a better system was devised. Similar installations were also made ready at Granton and, in February 1848, they were ordered to be retained.

Bouch's answer was both simple and imaginative, the floating railway. This comprised three main elements, an inclined pier at the dockside, a flying bridge to the vessel's deck and a flat deck on board the boat, lined with rails. The inclined pier had two standard gauge tracks upon which rested a moveable framework, cantilevered seawards and running on 24 wheels, six per rail, down the pier. The framework was substantial, 61 feet long, 21 feet wide, and had a 35 feet bascule or linkspan at the seaward end. The whole device was rolled up and down the pier on 24 wheels to suit the state of the tides and so match the deck level on the boat. The movement of the tide could be as much as 20 feet, this and the swell of the river both being catered for by the hinged linkspan, operated by a steam winch from a jib on the framework to the deck, which could also absorb the vertical rise and fall. This became the outline for almost all subsequent train and car ferries for the next 150 years.

The vessel carried only goods wagons as it was considered dangerous to shunt passenger coaches on the flying bridge and, as the open deck could offer no shelter, too exposed for passengers. Bouch designed the port facilities and Thomas Grainger produced drawings for the ship, which was called a 'goods boat' at the time. The most involved aspect he had to consider was the location of the engine to power the paddles, which he overcame by positioning a separate engine at each paddle, so freeing the intervening deck space for the maximum number of lines of rail. In frugal style, Bouch put the wheelhouse on a spartan gangway located between the two paddle housings, and unprotected from the elements. The movement of these flat-bottomed boats must have been rather erratic, as the speed of one engine was matched to the other! Neither would they would be likely to have provided a smooth crossing, as the Forth did not treat such vessels kindly!

Bouch placed the proposals before the EP&DR Board and with its approval placed an order for what has been accepted as the world's first roll-on, roll-off ferry with Robert Napier and Sons of Govan, Glasgow. The plan was initially to use the ferry, named PS *Leviathan*, on the Tay crossing since that firth offered a shorter passage and was less prone to bad weather. Shortly after the delivery of the boat to Granton in September 1849 for final fitting out, Bouch wrote to Learmonth, who was by now the company Chairman, to tell him that the service would begin operation on the Granton to Burntisland crossing. The slipways on the Tay were smaller than the Forth and thus could accommodate smaller boats. The PS *Leviathan* was more suited to the Granton to Burntisland passage. A second boat, appropriately named PS *Robert Napier*, was being built by Napier, for the Tay.

The Directors were brought to Burntisland on the last Saturday in January 1850 to witness the trials of PS *Leviathan*. The presentation was a disaster as the flying bridge broke away from the slipway and rolled down towards the river, throwing two of the contractor's employees into the water. One was rescued, badly injured but the second, John Forsyth of Newcastle was killed. The demonstration was abandoned and resumed the following Wednesday, again at Burntisland.

On the second occasion, the Directors witnessed 12 trucks being safely loaded down the slipway in a time of seven minutes before their coach was also put aboard. They then became the first (but not the last) passengers to be carried across the Forth in their own carriage on board one of the goods boats. At Granton, the Directors watched the trucks being rolled expeditiously off the boat in three minutes, before they left the quayside for lunch at the Granton Hotel, under the chairmanship of John Anderson, contractor for the crossing.

Bouch's optimistic plans were not to be achieved on schedule, however, since the rather involved shore installations were not ready and he had to ask permission to withdraw PS *Leviathan* in February until the work was completed. It not until March 1850 that the PS *Leviathan* was plying the Forth to Burntisland. The Duke of Buccleuch was asked to pay for the moorings at Granton pier for the new ship, but declined, although he agreed to allow the company to construct them on his property. Captain Field was asked to report if new moorings were absolutely necessary.

PS *Leviathan* at 399 tons was the larger of the two ferries first employed on the routes, the PS *Robert Napier* being 243 tons. Their speed across the firth was five knots. Both boats were particularly manoeuvrable, having two independent

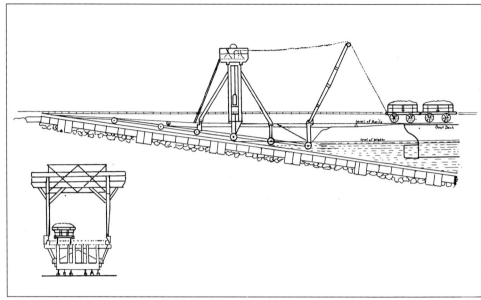

Sketch of Bouch's Floating Railway pier installation.   *Author*

PS *Auld Reekie* at the Prince Albert pier, Burntisland. PS *Carrier* at the Goods pier with two loaded wagons on board. The train shed of Burntisland station is visible in the background.
                                                    Douglas Yuill Collection

steeple engines driving the paddles. They each had a rudder at either end to further assist the manoeuvrability. This became more significant when it was found that wagons could easily run off the open end of the boat and blocks were installed to prevent this, effectively reducing the boat to a single-ended vessel.

When the second boat was placed in service, the possibility would then exist of sending goods and minerals from Edinburgh to Dundee 'without change of truck'. Loading and unloading, however, was not speedy with an average of 56 minutes for the complete crossing. One of the earliest journeys was to transport locomotives from the Granton line to the workshops at Burntisland for repair and the transfer of EP&DR locomotives to the southern shore for use on heavier trains. Two larger engines were sent for passenger trains and an 0-4-2 tender engine was sent to operate the Leith branch for either goods or passenger trains. Early recollections of old employees were that the lighter engines from the EL&GR were sent to Burntisland harbour lines to replace horse working, as several (equine) fatalities had occurred!

A short-lived agreement with the Scottish Central Railway in 1854 saw the temporary removal of goods boats from the Tay crossing to enable the carriage of goods to and from the North of Scotland to be routed via that company's tracks to Perth. However, the loss of revenue on both crossings was not attractive to the EP&DR and the arrangement only lasted for five years until 1859.

Further boats were built in later years as the service demanded. PS *Carrier*, 243 tons, was built at Greenock in 1858 and put on the Tay crossing, PS *Balbirnie*, 533 tons was built at Leith in 1861. Under NBR ownership (and employing the names of NBR Directors) there followed PS *Kinloch*, 585 tons, built in Glasgow, which entered service in 1865, and the final goods boat, PS *Midlothian* of 920 tons. The latter was also built at Leith but much later in 1881, when it became clear that the firths would not be bridged until the end of the decade. These boats provided an improved capacity, carrying an increasing number of wagons, from 20 wagons on the *Leviathan* to 40 on the *Midlothian*. By 1863, the PS *Balbirnie* was plying night and day, with two crews operating 12-hour shifts. Six crossings each way were undertaken in the full day with *Leviathan* acting as an auxiliary when required.

The PS *Carrier* was heralded in the Fife local press with a glowing description. She was fitted with 'non steaming oscillating engines' and a rudder at each end to enable her to steam either way over the river. The deck was laid with double length of rails and each trip would carry 'eight carriages'. This last remark is strange in that it suggests some carriages were transferred across the Forth. This may well have happened, since the men handling the rolling stock at either pier would have become more adept at transferring wagons and so carriages may have been the next step. In addition, carriages may have been transferred from one side of the Forth to the other for operational purposes. However, there is no indication that passengers remained in the carriages and may have travelled across separately.

It was certainly possible for passengers to make the crossing on a goods boat, for in February 1866, it was reported that the PS *Thane of Fife* had suffered a boiler explosion near Granton on the midday crossing. She limped back to port and passengers for the 2 pm ferry to the North were transferred to a goods boat.

Engraving of slipway at Granton showing 'Floating Railway'.   *James F. McEwan Collection*

Bouch's Floating Bridge on the Middle pier at Granton.   *Kirkcaldy Museum/3325A*

Certainly, anyone who arrived at Burntisland having missed the passenger steamer could cross on a goods boat at a reduced fare, if they could stand the privations of the open deck. An awning was ordered in 1875 'for one goods boat when used for passengers', and was intended to fit any of the goods boats. In 1868, PS *Dandie Dinmont* was moved from the Clyde to work the winter service on the Burntisland to Granton crossing, presumably as a relief boat as she then went to Tayport-Broughty Ferry in the summer months.

Despite the delays, the novel approach to ferry loading was a triumph, reducing the travelling time from Edinburgh to Dundee from up to two days prior to the railways to around 3½ hours. Bouch was able to report to the Board in March 1851 that the 'floating railway' was a complete success, having been in operation every single day since it began. In the first six months, 29,000 wagons had been transported over the Forth alone.

Accidents were, it must be supposed, inevitable with such advanced and intricate machinery. On Tuesday 3rd January, 1854, the weather was as might be expected on the Forth in the winter, a raging blizzard with snow falling heavily and lying on the ground, even at the river's edge. One of the goods boats was approaching Granton from Burntisland with a consignment of wagons. Locomotive No. 7, one of the original Edinburgh, Leith & Granton Railway stock, was approaching Granton pier, making ready to haul to wagons from the ferry. It was not apparent at the time if the points were wrongly set, or the snow had filled the gap, but the lightweight engine veered off the track towards the slipway, where the ferry was about to dock. The locomotive fell over the sea wall, ran down the slipway into the harbour waters, while the tender remained upright, having been checked by the sea wall, and stood alone on the slip. The driver and fireman leapt from the runaway engine and suffered only minor bruising. Observers noted that the slipway had a layer of ice beneath the snow, which assisted the progress of the engine towards the waters of the Forth.

Robert Geddes, the North British Engineer, was almost drowned in 1865 when working on the PS *Leviathan*. He had been inspecting work within the paddles when they were set in motion. He suffered severe facial injuries and was in a 'precarious condition' for several days. Described as an old and respected servant of the company, Geddes had been on the Granton to Burntisland crossing for many years having previously been with the private ferries.

The PS *Leviathan* was showing her age in 1878, after nearly 30 years transporting goods wagons across the Forth. Although by then relegated to a reserve boat, she was still in useful service whenever the need arose and the members of the NBR locomotive committee considered repairs to the vessel in the summer of that year. Having made a decision to dispose of the PS *Express* for scrap, the committee sought tenders to repair the original goods boat. Ramage and Ferguson offered to undertake the work for £2,100. The tender was accepted and the boat went to the Leith yard in November 1878. However, a strike of employees at the boatyard delayed completion and the NBR suggested that if the work was not resumed, then it would send its own men to the yard. By December, the NBR had sent 15 men to Ramage and Ferguson to complete the repairs, their wages being paid by that company.

Goods boat PS *Balbirnie* at Granton showing the rails over the Floating Bridge.
Kirkcaldy Museum/3324A

PS *Carrier,* showing the separate engines for each paddle and the spartan facilities on board.
Douglas Yuill Collection

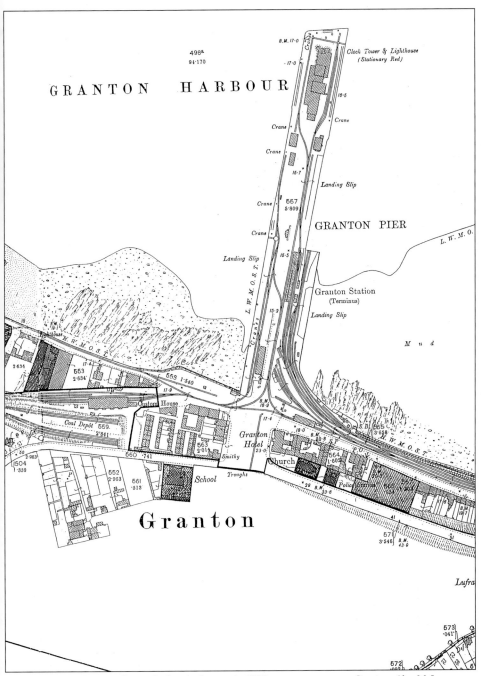

Granton Harbour as shown Ordnance Survey in 1895.   *Courtesy Alex McInnes*

Three goods boats tied up at Burntisland after withdrawal from service in 1890 (PS *Midlothian* on the right). *Douglas Yuill Collection*

In 1881, PS *Leviathan* was pressed into service to carry the Burntisland Militia to Holyrood Park in Edinburgh for what was to become to be known as the 'wet review'. Having traversed the river in both directions, with the men massed on deck, the boat ignominiously struck Burntisland pier and sank into the muddy waters. There was no loss of life and the troops were able to disembark safely, if somewhat damp, to provide the local residents with some choice language!

The Coalmasters

The Dunfermline branch of the Edinburgh, Perth & Dundee Railway between Crossgates and Dunfermline was opened on 13th December, 1849. The arrival of the Stirling & Dunfermline Railway from Alloa to Dunfermline on 28th August, 1850 prompted the operation of through trains, over the EP&DR's branch to Thornton and Burntisland, and provided an alternative route to Edinburgh. On the S&DR's opening, the Edinburgh & Glasgow refused to provide the motive power for the line and the company was forced to negotiate with the EP&DR to work its trains. Bouch made a proposal to the Board that the company charge 1s. 1d. per train mile to haul the S&DR coaches. This would exclude a further charge of £3 for the duties of a guard and any additional charges incurred through the Railway Clearing House (RCH). The RCH had been instituted to provide a common set of conditions for travel over more than one company's tracks.

The EP&DR had arrangements with most of the West Fife coalmasters to transport their output along the Dunfermline branch to Thornton and then round the coast to Burntisland. The eastern access from the main line to the docks added to the attractiveness of the handling of the coal wagons as they could be brought directly alongside the quay. The mineral wagons were initially entirely provided by the company, but their numbers soon became insufficient for an expanding coal output. The shortfall began to cause dismay amongst the coal owners, who depended on a good supply of wagons to transport their coal production, and complaints rained down on the EP&DR.

On 1st October, 1850, Mr Burn of Cuttlehill pit near Fordell wrote to the

EP&DR to complain of the 'lack of a supply of wagons' for his colliery. The company replied that it would do its best to keep a regular supply available but would not be liable for delays or expense that the colliery incurred. A dispute over the shortage of wagons seemed inevitable. The following month it became apparent that some coalmasters were holding out against the shortage of wagons and not paying their accounts. Christie of Townhill and Spowart of Wellwood and Balgonie had run up combined debts of £912. Spowart had another reason to complain as the Wellwood 'tramway' or branch line was not yet considered to be in a workable condition, and he was still carting coals to Dunfermline station. Once again, Bouch, as Manager at the time, was blamed and instructed by the traffic committee to put the branch into an operating state.

However, the EP&DR could not keep abreast of the demand for wagons and, in December 1850, the Lochgelly Iron and Coal Company wrote complaining of the shortage of wagons for its products. A similar complaint was received the same day from Mr Ballingall of the Balgonie Coal Company. The traffic committee began to fear that their trade was in jeopardy and wished to silence the complaints, which had become almost a daily occurrence. Their direction to Bouch to adopt a better system for the management of coal traffic was as much an admonishment of their Manager as it was an instruction. The committee stated that improvements could easily be achieved 'with very little attention to detail' on the part of Bouch. One of the members observed that wagons carrying stone were frequently delayed at Granton 'for want of a method of unloading them'.

Mr Tullis, a committee member, proposed that 500 additional wagons be procured, half to be provided by the company and half by the coal owners. The idea was remitted to James Ellis, the wagon shop foreman, for consideration but it is not clear whether or not the purchase was made. What is clear, however, is that the situation continued to worsen. Wagon repairs were also exacerbating the situation. In late January 1851, Nicholson was asked to report on the slow replacement of wagon wheels, and was instructed to order a further 500 wheels in malleable iron.

By then end of the first decade of operation, the coal business was developing well. Rates had been set as early as 27th October, 1847 at $1\frac{1}{2}d.$ per ton over 12 miles and $2d.$ per ton under 12 miles. In order to encourage trade from the coal owners of West Fife, the Dunfermline branch had been fixed lower at $1d.$ per mile. By 1860, pressure was mounting on the movement of coal because of the number of wagons in use and the number of wagons laid up for repair. On 2nd April, 1860, the Secretary, Henry Lees, wrote to following memorandum to all the coalmasters, to express the Directors' concern.

The number of waggons in use, if not sufficient for the present, is inadequate to accommodate larger traffic or afford means of development. As the Coal Owners are aware, the Company's means are limited and will not be able to provide sums equal to Coal Owners. So it is proposed that:

I.   Coal Owners purchase 150 Coal waggons to carry around $4\frac{1}{2}$ tons. The Edinburgh, Perth & Dundee Railway Company will provide an equal number of new waggons or waggons possessing equal capacity.

II.   Coal Owners to maintain their own waggons.

III.   The rate for Coal Owners waggons will be $\frac{1}{2}d.$ per mile per wagon.

IV.   Liability will be covered under Railway Clearing House rules.

Donibristle pit in 1833. This cost £10,000 to sink and £15,000 to fit out.   *Author's Collection*

The allocation to be:

I.   The Coal Owners to receive in their daily allocation, a number of the Company's waggons equivalent to the number or tonnage capacity of his own waggons at disposal on the same day; besides receiving the waggons belonging to himself also then at disposal.

II. Each his proportion of the Company's waggons remaining for allocation, inclusive of unconsigned foreign waggons.

III. Consigned foreign waggons to be disposed of as consigned.

Reduction in rates equal to   3¼*d*. per ton to Edinburgh
                                 4*d*. per ton to Tayport
                                 4¼*d*. per ton to Perth

The Coal Owners should decide the proportion of new waggons which each is to provide. The Company recommends:

Balgonie	10 waggons
Cluny	10 waggons
Cardenden	10 waggons
Cuttlehill	35 waggons
Donibristle	10 waggons
Dundonald	10 waggons
Dysart	10 waggons
Fordell	10 waggons
Halbeath	10 waggons
Lochgelly	50 waggons
Wellwood	20 waggons

It is not essential to the scheme that all Coal Owners concur with these proposals.

In view of the recurring shortages, the final statement is most surprising.

The Railway Clearing House rules mentioned in Lees' memorandum stated that responsibility for the wagons rested with the company in possession, except if the wagons were faulty in workmanship or materials, when the responsibility reverted to the owners.

Railway companies the country over were planning the biggest transportation of passengers that there had ever been when the Great Exhibition opened in 1851. Forward thinking Captain Mark Huish, of the London & North Western Railway (LNWR), wrote to the EP&DR with suggested rates for travelling to London. Lees, the Secretary, was happy to encourage the excursion traffic but wanted to ensure that the company covered its costs. He was instructed to ask for an allowance of 1s. per passenger, as there was no opportunity to recover the greater expense of handling passengers at the starting point of the journey.

Traffic increased both on the minerals and passenger sides of the business. During week ending 9th January, 1859, passenger, parcels and mail receipts amounted to £1,661 17s. 1d. while that for goods and livestock amounted to £1,547 4s. 6d. an increase of £91 17s. over the same week in the previous year.

Robert Nicholson was now established as locomotive superintendent at Burntisland works and had enough faith in his men to commence building locomotives for the company in 1861, reversing the earlier decision to put capital expenditure out to contract. The first of these locomotives was a 2-2-2 express passenger engine with inside frames and six-foot driving wheels. This was followed by four 0-6-0 engines, the first being completed in November 1861 and the second by January 1862. They were numbered 40 and 35 respectively and were built 'to replace two small Granton engines broken up'.

Activity on the other two engines, Nos. 49 and 50, was slow and by July 1862, only £700 worth of work had been done on them. The NBR, by now the owning company, showed in the half-yearly shareholders' report that one new goods engine was completed in the six months to January 1863 and one in the six months to July 1863. These two may not have carried their EP&DR numbers and would have been taken into the NBR as 159 and 160 (*see Appendix One*).

Thomas Bouch, always seeking new challenges, had resigned from the EP&DR in April 1851 to become an independent consulting engineer, setting up at 1 Hanover Street, Edinburgh. His expertise was being sought by small railway enterprises, keen to take advantage of his proposals to build and operate cheap railways.

Later Locomotives of the EP&DR

(The following is based on the notes of the late James F. McEwan.)

On 15th April, 1853, the company minutes record that a tracing was laid on the table, to convert the engines working on the Edinburgh, Leith & Granton section to do away the tender, the Sheriff having objected to engines working tender first. However, there is no evidence of this ever being carried out. In February 1854, it was agreed to purchase an extra engine for this section and Nicholson was authorised to buy two second-hand engines offered by the Lancashire & Yorkshire Railway at Manchester, if they were found suitable. There were not and Nicholson reported in September that the 'second-hand four wheeled engine on sale at Hartlepool was unsuitable.'

On 25th March, 1855, it was finally agreed to buy two large and one small engine forthwith, the former six-wheel goods engines at £2,100 and one four-wheel passenger locomotive at £1,550 all from Hawthorn's of Leith. The invoice date of the 0-4-0 was 24th December, 1855, the ledger adding in pencil 'supposed to be No. 43 engine' which suggests that the Granton locomotives had been incorporated into the EP&DR stock and renumbered by this time. No. 43 was sent to the Granton line. The invoice dates for the two 0-6-0s were 22nd January and 29th February, 1856, the first entered as No. 44 and the second No. 45.

Between 1st February, 1856 and 30th April, 1857, the EP&DR was worked by the Scottish Central Railway under a working arrangement supervised by a joint locomotive committee. During this time, the company operated 45 engines (including 10 on the EL&GR), 28 passenger and 17 goods. At 31st July, there were only 44 since No. 38 had been converted into a stationary engine to work the cables on the Granton slipway.

On 27th August, 1857, Robert Nicholson submitted a specification for an outside-cylinder six-foot single passenger locomotive. It was agreed to recommend to the newly formed Kinross-shire Railway (KR) that they took one of this type and that 'a new similar engine' replace No. 38. The new engine was not ordered, instead repairs were authorised for two engines. Hawthorn's estimates of £626 for No. 21 and £571 for No. 17 were accepted.

Two new 0-6-0 goods engines were ordered at £2,340 each from Neilson of Glasgow on 17th October, 1860. They were charged to the company in July 1861 and were numbered 38 and 46. (McEwan speculates that the engines were originally outside-cylinder 0-4-2s as the details were changed early in 1861 and the engines emerged as 0-6-0s.)

The Edinburgh, Perth & Dundee Railway entered into arrangements with minor mineral lines in the West of Fife and two of these were worked by EP&DR engines. The Leslie Railway (LR) was a short branch from Markinch to the town of Leslie to the west. EP&DR No. 47 appears to have worked this line although when it opened that company provided its own motive power until the 'new engine they have ordered is delivered', as the joint committee minute books show. The LR paid Hawthorn's of Leith, the builders of No. 47, in four instalments of £487 10s. The engine was therefore not shown in the EP&DR capital accounts.

The Kinross-shire Railway opened on 20th June, 1860, the KR Board having taken Nicholson's advice and ordered an engine from Hawthorn's in April, expecting delivery on 31st August, 1860. Robert Nicholson, took delivery of No. 48 at Burntisland at the end of 1860. After a trial period, he certified its worthiness and the engine passed to the KR who were duly invoiced by Hawthorn's on 14th January, 1861.

The St Andrews Railway (SAR), a 4½ mile branch from near Leuchars to the university town was engineered by Bouch as part of what came to be known as 'The Cheap Railway Movement'. This line was also worked by the Edinburgh, Perth & Dundee Railway, which supplied the rolling stock and motive power. A description of an accident to an 0-4-2 locomotive on the line on 16th May, 1864 suggests that one of the early Hawthorn engines was involved.

In its final returns before the NBR took over the company, the Edinburgh, Perth & Dundee Railway showed 20 passenger engines and 18 goods engines plus 4 four-wheelers on the Granton section with the two new goods engines under construction at Burntisland.

Chapter Four

The North British Railway

Consolidate to Survive

The original NBR line was formed between Edinburgh and Berwick, with a branch to Haddington and opened on 18th June, 1846. However, the NBR had aspirations beyond Edinburgh. Various amalgamations with adjacent lines including the Edinburgh & Dalkeith Railway as well as the Edinburgh & Glasgow and the Union Canal produced a strong competitor to the Caledonian Railway. The close association of the North British and the E&NR at the outset of the latter has already been mentioned, but the NBR was intent on capturing the borders' railways for itself. These lines were sponsored and then taken over by the North British, encouraged by its expansive Chairman, Richard Hodgson. While concentrating its attention on the South East however, the NBR had not ignored the 'kingdom' of Fife.

By the 1860s, the North British Railway sought to strengthen its position on the East Coast of Scotland and the route to the North. Concurrently, the Edinburgh, Perth & Dundee Company had sunk into a difficult financial position and did not pay a dividend in 1861-2. The company, along with others, became vulnerable to the predatory NBR and was soon to fall. Rumours of merger abounded in railway circles during the summer of 1861 and, by September, simultaneous meetings of the two companies shareholders were held in Edinburgh to announce their proposed union, taking the name of the North British Railway. The EP&DR shareholders would come a poor second in the new arrangement receiving less than half the dividends offered to the NBR shareholders. However, they ought to have considered themselves fortunate to receive anything when the parlous financial position of their company was revealed. The EP&DR shareholders were not happy with the prospect but the Board had secured sufficient proxies to force the decision through by 7,321 votes.

An Act of Parliament followed on 1st August, 1862 to bring about the end of the Edinburgh, Perth & Dundee Railway as it was incorporated into the North British fold. The same day the NBR route to Carlisle through the borders was inaugurated, an aspect of the NBR's growth which was considered to be more significant. The success was claimed as a personal triumph by Richard Hodgson who presided that evening at a celebration dinner for shareholders held in Carlisle.

The gaps in the East Coast route from Edinburgh to Aberdeen were putting the North British Railway at a disadvantage to the Caledonian, which had a slightly longer route in mileage but a simpler one without the two major firths to cross by ferry. The employees at Burntisland works must have speculated on the possibility of bridging the Tay when they were taken on a day excursion to Dundee in July 1864. It was reported in the *Fifeshire Advertiser* that Baxter Park, then a local beauty spot, was chosen as a destination since many of the men were 'connected with that town'. The train was 27 carriages long (!), leaving Burntisland at 8.00 am and returning to the town about 12 hours later.

EP&DR Hawthorn 0-6-0 locomotive.   *Author's Collection*

NBR 0-6-0 No. 159A, formerly EP&DR locomotive No. 49, begun at Burntisland in 1862 and completed there by the NBR.   *Author's Collection*

The initial impetus to improve the NB's service came from Dundee town council who pressed the NBR to reduce the journey time from the town to Edinburgh. The EP&DR had maintained a love-hate relationship with the neighbouring Scottish Central Railway with which it competed for traffic north of Edinburgh throughout its independence. The SCR had the benefit of traffic either from the Edinburgh & Glasgow route via Stirling or from the EP&DR itself direct into Perth through the Moncrieff tunnel. It had gone on to absorb the Dundee, Perth & Aberdeen Railway Junction in 1863, bringing Dundee and Aberdeen even closer to the Caledonian empire. The Caledonian Railway, however, acquired the SCR in 1865 and so was in a position to exercise some influence on the NBR's decision to bridge the firths.

The new owners of the route through Fife took the opportunity to put some of its existing locomotives on the northern route. One of the locomotives transferred to work the EP&DR lines from Burntisland is worthy of closer attention. NBR No. 55, a 2-2-2 that had started life as an entirely different and unique engine, was built in 1849 by E.B. Wilson, Leeds Railway Foundry for use on the North British main line to Berwick. It was a 2-2-2-0 Crampton design, and cost £2,800. It was altered at Stephenson's in 1855 and rebuilt in 1864 as a 2-2-2, retaining its boiler, only to be completely rebuilt along with some of the NBR's Hawthorns at St Margaret's in 1867. In this guise, it was reputed to be the fastest locomotive on the NBR. Latterly, it was based at Perth and occupied on the Perth to Ladybank trains.

Bouch's dream of bridging the Forth and the Tay seemed about to be realised when approval was given to build the first structure over the Forth. Parliamentary agreement was reached for a slender and spectacular bridge over the river upstream between Blackness and Charlestown; work began soon afterwards. An experimental pier, probably designed by Bouch, was built in November 1864, but it was two years later when the scheme to bridge the river appeared to start in earnest.

On Thursday 14th June, 1866, the population of Burntisland, along with many other visitors who arrived by the midday train and the Granton steamer, turned out to watch the launch of a massive raft. The structure was then towed to the site off Charlestown where it was to form the basis of a brick tower and create the first pier of the bridge. NB Directors, including George Kinloch, accompanied Thomas Bouch to the water's edge. Edgar Gilkes of the Middlesborough company which was erecting the structure and Baillie Falshaw of Edinburgh joined Leslie, the civil engineer who was responsible for the Burntisland pier works, with the rest of the party.

Once finished and filled with 10,000 tons of iron, the pier was intended to settle on the riverbed. The pier was on the point of completion, when a group of NBR Directors visited the site on 3rd August, 1866 and stopped all construction, discharging the builders. The company was in acute financial difficulties leading to a shareholders' revolt which in turn resulted in a wholesale clearance of many of the Board, Hodgson being forced to resign as Chairman. The massive raft was towed back to Burntisland where it remained before being taken back to North East England. Here its history becomes vague for it was either dismantled and removed to Gilkes' yard at Middlesbrough from where it was sold for scrap, or incorporated in the building of Redheugh bridge over the Tyne.

The Boardroom debacle was compounded when John Beaumont, a landowner from Huddersfield, was appointed Chairman and on 21st December, 1866 was given approval to invite John Stirling, Laird of Kippenross, to join the Board as a Director. Stirling had been associated with many of the Scottish railway schemes of the 1850s and 1860s having sold the Scottish North Eastern Railway to the Caledonian in 1865. Immediately on Stirling's appointment, Beaumont resigned to become Vice Chairman and proposed Stirling as Chairman, putting a Caledonian man at the head of the North British Railway!

Bouch's Tay Bridge

John Stirling continued Hodgson's enthusiasm for the need to bridge the two firths. Thomas Bouch produced a design for the Tay Bridge, so delicate that it caught the Victorian imagination. Following several false starts due to the failure of contractors, the work began on the two-mile crossing, the rest of the story surrendering to the history books.

However, the opening of the bridge on Friday 31st May, 1878 saw celebrations which could not have been imagined. Several trains were laid on to bring those paying tribute to the great new edifice. Over 1,500 people travelled to Dundee by train that day, but the most important train was that carrying the official party from Burntisland. The special left Edinburgh at 10 o'clock to join the PS *John Stirling* at Granton. The party left Burntisland in a train hauled by class '157' 0-4-2T No. 314 which brought the party through Fife to Leuchars. There they were joined by the Dundee party, which had arrived from Tayport. Around 1,500 passengers then crossed the Tay Bridge for the opening ceremony by Provost James Cox of Dundee at Tay Bridge station. The class '157' locomotive was one of a class of six that was intended for the intermediate stopping services from Dundee once the bridge had been opened. As a celebration of the new services across the Tay Bridge, the class was named in 1879 after locations associated with the route.

| No. 88 | *Kirkcaldy* | No. 89 | *Ladybank* | No. 157 | *Markinch* |
| No. 167 | *Dundee* | No. 314 | *Lochee* | No. 480 | *Burntisland* |

These names were painted on the side tanks, in keeping with the NBR tradition. All six of the class were rebuilt as 0-4-4Ts from 1881.

The Drummond tank was not destined to attain the celebrity of the locomotive which hauled the final train over the bridge. Just over 18 months later stormy weather on the Tay made victims of a large section of the completed bridge and the lives of 75 passengers on 28th December, 1879.

On that stormy Sunday, the 4.15 pm mail train left Edinburgh as normal to travel to Granton, where the passengers transferred to the *John Stirling** or the choppy crossing to Burntisland pier. On the northern shore, a train of five coaches and brake van waited at the platform in Burntisland station, a short walk from the pier. The train had already formed the 1.30 pm Dundee to Burntisland and was about to return at 5.20 pm. The turbulent weather continued as the passengers made their way from pier to station to board the coaches, a four-wheel third class, a six-wheel first and two further thirds, followed by a second class vehicle and the brake van.

* Some sources have this as the PS *William Muir*.

The locomotive was No. 224, a 4-4-0 designed by Thomas Wheatley and one of two built at Cowlairs in 1871 for express passenger duties on the route through Fife. No. 224 and her sister, No. 264 spent almost all their early days in Fife, but No. 224 was not the rostered locomotive for the train, having been relegated at the time to spare engine at Dundee. The Drummond tank, No.89 Ladybank, which would normally have take the train was suffering from a breakdown and so driver David Mitchell and fireman John Marshall set forth at 5.27 pm on the footplate of the green Wheatley. The train kept good time, even more necessary with 14 scheduled stops before Dundee and a howling gale blowing. Only a little late at Thornton, the train was at Leuchars by 7.00 pm only a few miles from home. At the final stop, St Fort, the tickets were collected from the passengers before they set off over the bridge and their deaths.

The telegram, sent by station master James Smith of Dundee Tay Bridge station to the North British headquarters in Edinburgh, has entered the annals of railway history:

> Terrible accident on the bridge.
> One or more of High Girders blown down.
> Am not sure as to the safety of last train from Edinburgh.
> Will advise further as soon as can be obtained.

Later that evening, fireman George Wilkie was on board the pilot engine which was taking wagons from the Granton goods boat at Burntisland, when he noticed a well dressed figure hurry from the open deck and onto the pier. As he passed the locomotive, Wilkie heard the man ask an inspector on the platform, 'Is it true that the bridge is down?' On receiving an affirmative reply, the now knighted Sir Thomas Bouch disappeared into the darkened station, clearly upset that his bridge had fallen. The Chairman and Directors were alerted to the news and arrangements were immediately made for them to travel to Dundee early on the morning of Monday 29th December.

A special train left Edinburgh at 12.20 am, the party crossing from Granton on the goods boat, PS *Leviathan*, to Burntisland where a second special train took them to Leuchars. The group, which included John Stirling and John Walker were joined at Burntisland by Bouch, arriving at four o'clock to be met by Thomas Robertson, the station master. Mistakenly, they were told that 300 had perished and this figure was reported back to Edinburgh. However, the count of tickets revealed that 75 passengers and crew had been killed when the 5.20 pm from Burntisland had been thrown into the Tay.

With the fall of the Tay Bridge, Fife was once more a North British island, cut off from both the North and the South. The long sought through route from London to the North now had two breaks in it again. With the Tay Bridge in use, the NB had pushed its share of the traffic to Dundee to 85 per cent but this now fell to 51 per cent. Work had already begun on another of Bouch's designs, a double suspension bridge over the Forth at Inchgarvie, authorised on 5th August, 1873. Under the circumstances, it was inevitable that the work stopped immediately and shortly after Bouch had retired to his home in Moffat, where he later died, the contracts for the Forth Bridge were formally terminated. The Tay and the Forth would assuredly be bridged but not by one of Bouch's fragile designs.

Forth Bridge

As a Bill to abandon the Forth Bridge was before Parliament, moves were begun to ensure that the river was bridged. On 11th June, 1881, interested railway companies met at York to discuss financing a more robust structure for the Forth, indeed one which would become a wonder of the age. The group which was known, at first, as the Forth Bridge Railway Committee later formed a separate company to build and to operate the bridge. The North British contributed 35 per cent, the Midland Railway (MR) 30 per cent and 17½ per cent each by the North Eastern Railway (NER) and Great Northern Railway (GNR). The NBR was responsible for building the approach tracks on either shore and improving some of the lines, including a new direct route from Perth to Queensferry and another from Burntisland to Inverkeithing.

John Fowler and Benjamin Baker were invited to draw up a new design for the bridge and William Arrol was contracted to build the structure, now much more heavily engineered than the doubtful Bouch projects. Arrol also won the contract to build the new bridge over the Tay (and Tower Bridge, all at the same time). The giant cantilever design required over 54,000 tons of steel, 640,000 cubic feet of granite from Aberdeen and 62,000 cubic feet of masonry. It is sad to relate that John Stirling, Laird of Kippenross, who had guided the North British from its shadowy days of financial impropriety to acclaim for its Tay Bridge, died at the end of July 1882, before he had seen both firths safely bridged. The new Forth Bridge had received its Royal Assent on 12th July, 1882.

However, the bridge was not sufficient in itself to complete the connection from Edinburgh to Dundee, to Perth and to Aberdeen. New lines had to be laid on the south side from the Edinburgh & Glasgow line at Saughton and a completely new railway was created through Fife, linking North Queensferry to Perth and the North. A branch had been opened from Dunfermline to the port at North Queensferry on 1st November, 1877 to connect with the ferry there, but passenger services ended on 5th March, 1890, the day after the opening of the new bridge. A long held ambition to reach Perth from West Fife was realised when a line linking Cowdenbeath, Kinross and Perth opened.

All the attention of the engineering and public press was naturally focused on the massive creation, which became the Forth Bridge, but the approach lines were impressive in their own way. The Edinburgh & Northern route was not ignored but the resulting route meant that Burntisland would lose its position as terminus for the railway service through Fife. The contract for eight miles of double track was let to John Waddell for £140,000. Threading the rails westward from Burntisland was not a simple task and presented the engineers with a challenge to negotiate a path between the existing station building, which was at the level of the harbour, and the higher ground beyond Rossend Castle. The ensuing gradients are 1 in 94 eastwards and 1 in 100 westwards.

As we saw in an earlier chapter, Burntisland town council had raised objection to rails crossing the High Street on the level. To overcome the problem, a dramatic alteration in the profile of the railway at Burntisland was required. The route diverged to the landward side from the line into the harbour and was taken on a rising 12-chain curve from Lammerlaws Bridge, behind and above the existing station. The curve through Burntisland station has required a speed limit of 25 mph ever since.

There had previously been rock removal when the first station was built at the port and the extension necessitated the removal of further rock and the demolition of several old buildings. The new line was built over a siding to the north of the station and a few feet above it. The new platforms therefore sat higher than above the original building and just to the north. Then the line broke out on to a viaduct that crossed at the western end of the High Street, the sharp curve over Harbour Place avoiding the sidings to the north of the West dock. The entrance was through the existing building with a subway to the down platform.

However, the new alignment impinged upon the buildings, which lay along the route and so necessitated the demolition of several of them. The outlook for those people living at the western end of the High Street was dramatically altered. Two public houses were amongst those buildings that were demolished, the Royal Hotel and McArthur's Steamboat Tavern, although replacements were constructed at either end of the iron girder viaduct. The basement of the Steamboat had a large rock jutting into the cellar which is part of the viaduct foundations, maintaining stability

The construction of the bridge and the approach lines brought a new generation of 'navvies' to the area, employed by John Waddell, the contractor for the approach lines. The life of the navvy on the Aberdour section was recorded in *The Dunfermline Journal* on 20th October, 1888. Titled 'Hut Life on the Aberdour and Burntisland Railway', the account painted a graphic illustration of the way of life of the men building the line from Inverkeithing to Burntisland. More of an existence, they lived in specially constructed huts, which were made of wood and comprised a dining hall, kitchen and sleeping apartments. The dormitories had iron beds, each for two people, ranged along either side. Around 30 to 40 men could be accommodated at a charge of 4d. per evening. They cooked their own food in the hut at Aberdour.

Breakfast was from 6.00 am to 7.00 am each day and the rush of 150 men to the store can be imagined. Only one hot plate was provided and the scramble meant that many men left for a day's work without hot food. Even worse was the time allowed for dinner in the evening. Only 30 minutes was permitted for the men to prepare their evening meal and so many remained content with bread and butter and a jug of beer. Some would have a scone instead of bread, the more adventurous placing a piece of raw meat within the scone, which gained the nickname of a 'push-by'.

The quality of food and of its preparation was not of the highest order and so the meals were far from appetising. It was little wonder that more time was spent in the consumption of drink than wholesome food. As meals had to be over by 6.30 pm, most evenings and especially Saturdays were spent drinking cheap beer or spirit. Sunday was generally a rest day and was spent out of doors, but a religious service was held in the dining hall, generally over the babble of voices of those who were not participating.

The first step in the restoration of the NBR's fortunes occurred on 20th April, 1887 when the new Tay Bridge was opened and trains once more could run from Burntisland to Dundee and beyond, 'without change of truck' as Bouch had described it in reference to his goods boats. The final link over the Forth, producing the greatest bridge that the world had then seen, was completed on 14th November, 1889. The unsurpassed design stood alone, supported by its own internal stresses and resistant to wind and temperature changes.

The opening of the Forth Bridge on 4th March, 1890 was performed by the Prince of Wales. A cold, squally day with driving rain, so typical of the capricious weather on the firth. With sailors positioned across the bridge and a salute from a naval ship below in the river, the Royal Train crossed the magnificent structure from Dalmeny to North Queensferry. On its return trip, the train stopped on the bridge to allow the Prince to insert the final rivet, as the wind blew around the party, flapping at coats and grabbing hats from the heads of the distinguished guests. Traffic did not begin to cross the bridge until 1st June and even then, it was limited to 40 mph. However, success was guaranteed, for the opening immediately reduced the journey time of scheduled trains from Kings Cross to Aberdeen by one hour to 13 hours.

Having seen railway races to Edinburgh in the summer of 1888, it was perhaps surprising that the East Coast and West Coast companies did not break rank from their agreements and begin a new challenge to reach Aberdeen first. However, racing did begin once more in 1895, when Fife saw a nightly train race to Dundee and the effective winning post at Kinnaber Junction north of Montrose. Although the NBR engines did their best, the Caledonian claimed victory on the night of 23rd August, cutting the journey from London down to eight hours 23 minutes, by running special trains with few coaches.

Closer to Burntisland, the opening of the bridge meant the closure of the ferry, at least in part, a situation that had a series of consequences for the town. There was an immediate reduction in the number of men employed on the crossing as well as those at the passenger terminal and station. The locomotive depot was less significant since trains no longer began their journeys from Burntisland. Economically, the burgh of Burntisland had possibly seen the best of its days. With fewer passengers visiting in the town, the hotel trade diminished, commercial business was severely hit and the importance of the town as a destination lessened.

Fortunately, the coal export trade continued to expand and, as we shall see in Chapter Five, soon outgrew the harbour facilities. Burntisland did capitalise on its sandy beach and with sea bathing becoming an accepted practice, developed a holiday trade which took advantage of the town's hotels and flourished into the 20th century. One consequence of the new bridge for Edinburgh was the resultant congestion at Waverley station as the traffic to West and North grew dramatically.

Although under the control of the locomotive foreman at Burntisland, Thornton Junction was now a more significant location for basing locomotives, being on the main line and at the crossroads of lines to West Fife, East Fife and the Wemyss private railway. Twenty locomotives were based there in 1890 to handle the Forth Bridge traffic. The first goods train after the bridge opened, direct from Thornton to Leith Walk was worked by a Wheatley 0-6-0, No. 413.

Locomotives were transferred to Thornton from both Burntisland and Ladybank, in addition to a number from Dundee. Thornton's facilities consisted of a coaling shed and stage with a hand crane for coaling locomotives, two short sidings adjacent, one for the turntable and the other for disposal of ash, etc. The development of the Wemyss system and of the Fife coalfield forced the pace of expansion at Thornton. Methil No. 2 dock was opened in part in 1897 and Burntisland East dock opened in 1901, both of which caused strain on Thornton's resources.

Direct Lines

Indeed, so busy was the route from West Fife to Burntisland via Thornton, that there were several proposals to build a more direct line from the Cowdenbeath and Dunfermline pits to the port.

Around 1874, Robert Underdown, the General Manager of the Manchester, Sheffield & Lincolnshire Railway submitted a statement to a Parliamentary committee, which not only failed to uphold the case for the line but also vindicated the status quo and the potential of the existing routes. By comparing the proposed line with those in South Yorkshire, he tried to show the expensive nature of the planned undertaking. His fascinating statement reads:

Robert George Underdown will prove

That he is General Manager of the Manchester, Sheffield & Lincolnshire Railway Company, which position he has held during a period of 15 years past.

That he has been over the existing Lines in Fifeshire belonging to the North British Company and that he has made himself acquainted with the route of the proposed mineral line.

Is of the opinion that such proposed line is badly and inconveniently laid out not only from an engineering point of view, but also with regard to the working or development of the traffic of the district.

That in its main feature, it is a duplication of existing lines of the North British Company without corresponding advantage.

That the gradients are so severe as will cause the proposed Railway not only to be unprofitable, but dangerous to work.

Is of opinion that should the future development of the traffic of the district require more Railway facilities, the existing Fifeshire lines of the North British Company are conveniently laid out either for extension or provision of additional lines and sidings and That the gradients are such as cause no serious obstacle to the proper and safe working of the traffic.

That on similar lines under Witness' own management in the South Yorkshire Coal District there are one or two short branches having heavy gradients which are found to be most inconvenient to work and which Witness will explain - For instance - on the Grange Colliery branch used exclusively for Mineral Traffic, the gradients are 1 in 50 for a distance of 1 mile 882 yards and 1 in 32 for a distance of 1 mile and 395 yards upon which the maximum load is 12 wagons for one of the most powerful engines.

Also on the Barnsley Branch with its junction to the South Yorkshire Line, the gradients are 1 in 67 for a distance of 1 mile 121 yards and 1 in 50 for a distance of 1 mile and 154 yards, the maximum load for the same kind of engine as in the previous case being 15 wagons.

MAP 3.

MINING.

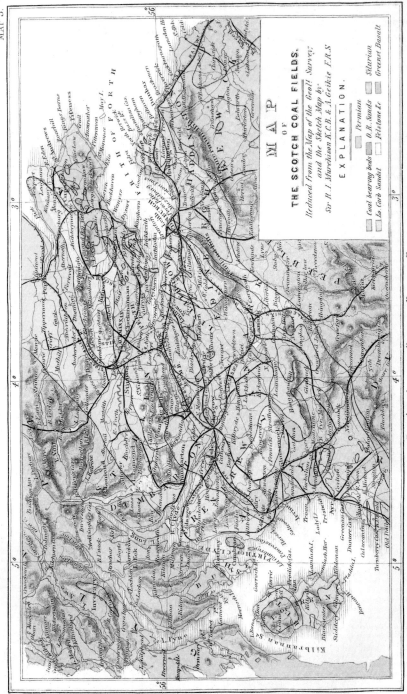

MAP
OF
THE SCOTCH COAL FIELDS.

Reduced from the Map of the Geol! Survey,
and the Sketch Map by
Sir R. I. Murchison K.C.B. & A.Geikie F.R.S

EXPLANATION.

Coal bearing beds	Permian
La Carb Sandst	O.R. Sands
	Pitstone &c
	Silurian
	Greenst Basalt

English Miles

WILLIAM MACKENZIE, LONDON, EDINBURGH, GLASGOW

Upon those branches in addition to the powerful ten ton Brakes used, sprags have also to be resorted to as an auxiliary to the brake and in this way it frequently happens that two thirds of the total number of wagons on the train have to be spragged which necessitates extreme caution on the part of the working staff to avoid mishap.

Witness shall explain that these branches form part of a system belonging to the South Yorkshire Railway Co. which was transferred to the Manchester, Sheffield & Lincolnshire Railway Company some 10 years ago.

Witness will further explain that if it be urged on the part of the direct Mineral Line that two brakes might be used that it would be most inconvenient in as much as on arrival to a terminus one of the brakes would have to be disposed of before the wagons could be dealt with and even if this were practicable it would add to the already heavy expense and difficulty of working the line.

He will explain the basis upon which rates of Coal are arranged from Collieries in the South Yorkshire District and the minimum rate his Company is empowered to charge and is being charge, for conveyance over the South Yorkshire for further transit.

Uniform charge made in South Yorkshire for Coal to Doncaster for Great Northern Company - the average is taken as 16 miles and the charge agreed to is 1s. 4d. per ton.

To the junction with the Midland at Swinton which is about 7 or 8 miles nearer to most of the collieries, the charge is 3/17ths less.

Minimum rate of 1s. per ton for same distance via the South Yorkshire line.

Witness is of the opinion that the rates charged by the North British Company are reasonable.

Witness will further explain that it is not customary for his company to provide wagons for Coal traffic, such wagons being supplied either by the Colliery Companies or by the Coal Merchants themselves.

Is of the opinion the difficulties of working the traffic at Burntisland as proposed by the promoters will be very great.

The NBR raised a Bill in Parliament in 1875 for the creation of a direct line from Burntisland to Cowdenbeath since their new dock (*see Chapter Five*) would require a regular flow of traffic from the West Fife coalfield. Included in the Bill were branches to all the collieries in the district, and of course, this meant negotiations with the coalmasters to agree to transfer their consignments to the new line. The coalmasters objected to the line because the NBR wanted to charge 1s. 6d. per ton for the journey, when the rate for Charlestown was 1s. 4d. per ton. The rate would then have been the same as that by Thornton, a much longer route. Negotiations with Burntisland magistrates had resulted in their consent to a different rate, but the coalmasters were not to be swayed and the Bill was withdrawn. Many familiar faces amongst the coal owners met the NBR Directors in March 1876 to seek agreement:

Lochgelly Iron and Coal Company
Cowdenbeath Coal Company
Donibristle Coal Company
Ord Adams   Proprietor of Hill of Beath Colliery
Andrew Wallace   Proprietor of Hallbeath Colliery
Townhill Coal Company
West of Fife Coal Company
Thomas Spowart and Company Proprietors of Wellwood and Elgin Collieries
Lassodie Colliery Company

Bill Lynn Collection

NBR 0-6-0 No. 87 ('J34') at Burntisland.

NBR class 'D' Holmes 0-6-0 No. 80 at Burntisland. Later LNER class 'J33'.
Peter Westwater Collection

It was then agreed by John Stirling, Chairman of the NBR, and Thomas Spowart of Broomhead, Dunfermline and Lauritz la Cour, a Director of Leith Iron and Coal Company, that the NBR would carry coals in its own wagons through Thornton to the harbour junction at Burntisland for 1s. 6d. per ton (1s. per ton in traders' own wagons). The rate to Charlestown would be identical. A reduction in the price of steam coal to 12s. 6d. per ton would see a reduction of 3d. per ton in carriage. The idea of a direct line was kept alive with a final clause, which stated that if the coalmasters were not satisfied with the arrangement after five years, the NBR would provide a more direct line to Burntisland than that through Thornton. A refusal by the NBR to honour this aspect would be subject to arbitration. Although a direct line was not built, a rather poor alternative was created out of the potential of Seafield, near Kirkcaldy, for a new harbour. The Kirkcaldy and District Railway, of which more later, was developed from a proposed branch at Invertiel and sufficed as a shorter route to Burntisland from the West Fife coalfield.

In the 1880s, Thornton was a sub-shed of Burntisland and still comprised only a coaling shed and stage with a hand-operated crane to transfer coal. The engines and men were responsible to the locomotive foreman at Burntisland. As coal traffic increased, pressure was exerted on the poor facilities and improvements became necessary. Once the Forth Bridge was built, the fortunes of the engine sheds at Burntisland and Thornton would be reversed.

Loading coal wagons onto a sailing ship prior to building of West dock.

Courtesy Edward Wilson

The Herring Craig Pier, Burntisland around the middle of the 19th century, lithographed by C. Schacher of Edinburgh from a calotype by Thomas Roger.   *St Andrews University Library*

Chapter Five

Harbour Developments

The North British Railway had succeeded in retaining its monopoly of railways in Fife, repelling its most determined competitor, the Caledonian, and so in the mid-1860s all seaward sales of coal continued to leave the county on NBR rails to the docks. There remained, however, one major thorn in the side of the NBR. The Wemyss family had owned land in East Fife since the Middle Ages and had developed coal mining in the area since the 17th century. Minor harbours at West Wemyss, Leven and Methil enabled exportation of this locally mined coal to foreign and domestic markets without the need to transport it long distances overland.

The Wemyss Coal Company was formed to work the coal measures and through negotiations with neighbouring coal owners and the North British Railway itself, eventually had its own extensive private railway. The history of the system is thoroughly recounted in a companion volume from Oakwood Press, *The Wemyss Private Railway*, by Alan Brotchie and needs no elaboration, save to remark that the relationship between Randolph Gordon Erskine Wemyss and the NBR, of which he became a Director, was not always cordial.

The harbour at Burntisland was soon to prove insufficient for the growth in shipping, which the port was experiencing only 10 years after the arrival of the railway. The extent of the port was just over seven acres with only 570 feet of quayside available for shipping. In 1855, 6,000 tons of coal were being exported per year and the expansion of the coalfields of Fife was progressing rapidly. During one week in 1860, seven foreign and one British owned vessel had departed from Burntisland with coal, a considerable traffic considering the somewhat primitive facilities that existed. The solitary arrival at the port during the same week was 800 tons of barley. However, one aspect of inward cargoes which reports ignored was those items brought over on the train ferries. These remained unquantified.

Advertisements appeared in the *Fifeshire Advertiser* in February 1858, seeking estimates to complete works at the breakwater at Burntisland. Later the same year, in October, there were progress reports in the newspaper on the general improvements to the harbour. The developments included the extension to the breakwater on the west side of the harbour by 500 feet, which now afforded protection to the south and the south-west. New loading berths constructed on the east side were well advanced and would permit drafts of nine feet at low tide and 24 feet at high tide.

The harbour was extended further from 1860 at a cost of £12,000 and, by June 1861, was reported as being complete. The 1861 improvements furnished new sheltered wharves to the seaward side of the existing port, 'new powerful cranes' being installed in 1862. Three berths were provided and a lighthouse, supplied by D.C. Mudie's Panmure works in Edinburgh, produced a 'bright red light'. Soon the additional work proved to be inadequate for the expansion of trade especially since the port still had no mechanised loading for coal.

The railway system was now settling down with more reliable and larger motive power and bigger wagons to transport coal. Coupled with better mining techniques, coal traffic placed ever-greater demands on the railway. A meeting of Burntisland town council on 1st August, 1865 was told that the North British proposed to create a deep-water harbour with the support of the coalmasters for their own use. It was intended to form the harbour on the east side of the pier, which was then in the course of erection. The council was asked to consider waiving the shore dues and believed that it should have compensation for the loss of revenue. Provost Sievewright was given authority to open negotiations with the railway company.

In 1872, it was reported that iron masters were experiencing difficulty in receiving their full supplies and all collieries were 'as fully employed as they care to be'. More pits were being sunk in Fife and all the county's ports were 'full of vessels waiting to be freighted' and complaints of the delay in procuring cargoes were 'not at all infrequent'. New docks proposed for Burntisland and West Wemyss could not come quickly enough.

The wagon shortage continued to dog the relations between railway and the coal masters. Both the North British Railway and the Caledonian Railway were caught up in the shortage at the beginning of 1872; the latter's solution being to purchase many more wagons and to take over the wagons of coal masters to spread distribution more evenly. An additional impediment to production for the coal masters was an ongoing dispute with miners over wages and their working week.

By 1873, the amount transhipped at Burntisland had reached 140,000 tons, and the North British saw it as a potential competitor to Methil. The battle would be for the output of the pits in the Auchterderran and Thornton region, which could be taken by rail to either port. Additionally, pressure remained high for a direct route from West Fife to Burntisland, for ironically, by transporting the coal to the port via Thornton, the North British Railway was inadvertently coming closer to Wemyss' port at Methil than Burntisland.

West Dock

The dock at Burntisland had to become more attractive to the coal owners and to offer a faster turnaround for their wagons in order to compete with the East Fife ports. On 5th November, 1872, the NBR ended an existing arrangement with the Burntisland town council and entered a new one to create a new dock of about 3½ acres alongside the existing facilities. It was not to prove the happiest of arrangements for the company as negotiations with Burntisland town council would, not for the first time, prove difficult.

The agreement was formalised in an Act, (35 & 36 Vict. cap. ccix) North British Railway Act of 1873, which also authorised the continuance of contracts made in the Corporation of Burntisland provisional order. This was made by the Board of Trade and confirmed under the Piers and Harbours Orders Confirmation Act 1870 (No. 3). The Burntisland town council demanded large sums from the NBR for harbour dues and burgh customs upon the termination of the existing October 1870 agreement in December 1872. Indeed plans were drawn up for the proposed dock as early as 1870, when Thomas Meik and William D. Nisbet, civil engineers of Sunderland, submitted proposals on 16th December that year. There was, however, a delay of a month before the original plan of Meik and Nisbet was approved by David Jackson, for the town council, and Walter Scott, the contractor.

One of the clauses of the schedule to the Act required the North British to relieve the Burntisland town council of the existing harbour debt not exceeding £10,000 and pay the interest from November 1872. Another clause was that the NBR would advance £50,000 to the town at five per cent. Further Acts (38 & 39 Vict. cap. c) in 1875 and (40 & 41 Vict. cap. lviii) in 1877 allowed for more cash to be contributed to the harbour works and to extend the time permitted to complete the construction, both the subject of much negotiation between the company and the council.

However, agreement was reached between the NBR and the town council and dated 7th and 17th September, 1874, the official documents being signed by a range of dignitaries mainly from the ranks of the town's councillors:

Adam Johnstone, NBR Solicitor
Alexander McKillop, clerk to the Solicitor
Baillie, Thomas Strachan
Dean of Guild, James Robertson
Councillor Robert Dover
Councillor William Inglis
Councillor Andrew McBryde
Councillor George Robertson
Councillor William McIntosh
Town Clerk, Thomas Alexander Wallace
Town Officer, Daniel McFeely

Thomas Bouch, now an independent engineer working from his office at York Place in Edinburgh, acted as the NBR's consulting engineer on the extension. Along with Thomas Meik and Sons, now also of York Place, Edinburgh, who had drawn up the plans, he presented regular reports to both the town council and the NBR. From the outset of the contract, Mr P.W. Meik was placed in charge as resident engineer. Thomas Meik himself later wrote a paper for *The Engineer* magazine in which he modestly commented that there was nothing novel in the construction of the dock and the harbour was only notable for the geological formations. Certainly, a great variety of minerals were excavated from the site, including coal, shale, hematite, barytes and calc-spar, 40 different minerals in all.

Seven separate contracts were let initially for the new dock, amounting to almost £70,000. These contracts included the physical excavation and construction of the dock, provision of the machinery, demolition of older properties and additional works such as road and drain laying and positioning rails. Construction of the dock progressed slowly and the expected completion date of the end of 1874 passed without the slightest chance of the work being finished. A minor setback occurred in January 1875 when it was reported by Burntisland town council to the NBR that a crack had appeared in the west wall

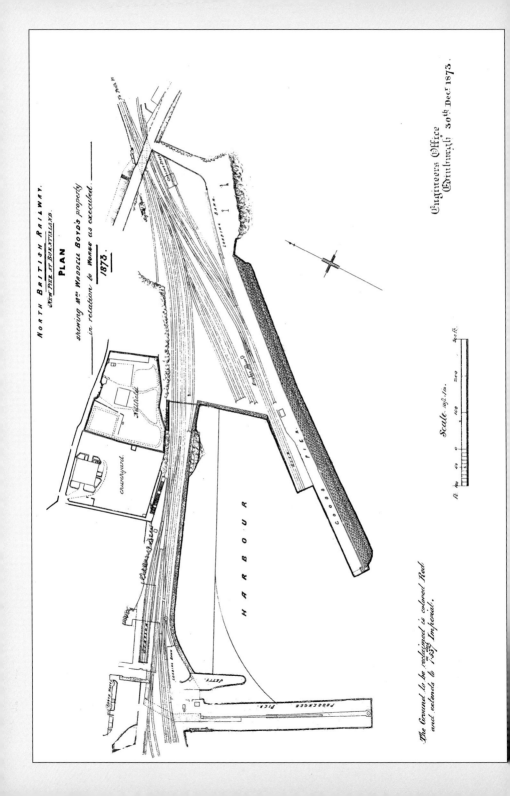

NORTH BRITISH RAILWAY.

NEW PIER AT BURNTISLAND.

PLAN

shewing Mrs Waddell Boyd's property
in relation to Works as executed.

1873

Engineers Office
Edinburgh 30th Dec. 1873.

The Ground to be redesigned is colored Red
and extends to 1·53 Imperial.

Scale 40 f.¹In.

HARBOUR

PASSENGER PIER.

JETTY.

PIER.

of the dock. Action was quickly taken to prevent further subsidence and, by the end of 1875, progress had reached the stage where water could be allowed to enter the partially finished harbour.

However, one significant aspect was that while the plans dealt admirably with the method of handling coal exports, there was a lamentable scarcity of provision for import trade, lacking even light cranes or storage sheds. Meik felt that it was doubtful that the council would approve the creation of these facilities once the work was complete. He related in his paper that the operations began on New Year's day, 1873 and that the plan was changed several times to 'meet the views of the different parties'. The erratic relationship between the town council and the railway was illustrated by his comment that works nearly stopped 'for want of concord between the bodies interested'.

Although the town council frequently argued with the NBR over many and various aspects of the dock and its construction, an agreement was eventually reached. The Burntisland councillors resented the necessity of handing over control of their important harbour to a railway company, especially one from Edinburgh. On the other hand, the NBR felt that it did not have any responsibility for funding the project in total since it would be replacing harbour facilities which already existed, albeit with a rather more substantial facility. The behaviour of the town council was commented upon later by the *Fifeshire Advertiser* in a leading article on 20th January, 1877. 'Burntisland Town Council wears its troubles like its honours, very lightly and conducts its affairs in some sort of way that defies opposition.'

In January 1876, the two engineers, Bouch and Meik, reported that since the admittance of water to the dock, little progress had been made, because of a problem with the watertight gates. Sir William Armstrong and Company of Elswick Works, Newcastle was responsible for provision of the dock gates as well as the hydraulic engines and hoists. The engineers suggested that once the water had been pumped out between the gates and the cofferdam, the task of advancing the construction should be given over 'to a competent person', presumably requiring a resident foreman to oversee the works.

They remarked on the remaining work with specifications and plans for the outstanding timberwork for the hoists, engine and boiler houses, the demolition of houses in Dock Street and for the building of roads and drains. The North British Railway was responsible for the erection of the goods shed on filled-up land of the old dock and for laying the rails. The rails were to become a subject for dispute with both the council and later with the coalmasters.

Financial affairs were also a bone of contention between the company and the council, with the NBR showing reluctance to release funds for each stage of the construction. For its part, the NBR put the blame for delays in ensuring the works progressed on Burntisland town council. The company believed the town was slow in forwarding the mortgage instalments, while the town council believed that the NBR was at fault for dragging its feet in paying the contractors. Letters passed between George Bradley Wieland, Secretary of the NBR and Thomas Wallace, town clerk of Burntisland. Wieland was informed that Walter Scott, the contractor for excavating the dock and erecting the masonry, had only 50 men on site and that it was looking likely that the completion would have to be postponed. At the same time, Wallace complained to Wieland that the first instalment of the company's loan (£50,000) was nearly exhausted and that no further contracts could be entered into until further sums were assured.

In mid-January 1876, Wieland confirmed that the NBR would provide extra funds but that it would not pay for the rails along the quaysides. Wallace was frustrated at this stance and went over Wieland's head by asking the Directors for their views on the plans. Meik and Bouch had approved the layout of the sidings but complained that they had not seen the proposals for the roads around the dock before these had been set out. The dispute over finances continued throughout the month. The estimate for rails within the harbour boundary was £3,000 with an additional £800 for turntables at the hoists. These small turntables allowed wagons to be towed by horse, from the adjacent siding to the hoist, for emptying into ships and then returned. In February, Wallace asked Wieland once again if the NBR would lend more to Burntisland town council at the same rates as the initial £50,000 approved in the 1872 Act.

The dispute continued during March and work on site stopped completely while the two sides sought to agree which party would pay for the rails. Meik added to the row by asking for payment for the extra work, seeking an additional five per cent of his fee. However, the rails for the dockside remained without a contractor. The railway and the town met on 24th April, 1876 when the NBR agreed to pay no more than £3,800 to lay the rails and confirmed its part of the agreement of November 1872.

By early May 1876, a new harbourmaster was appointed and further contracts were announced for the demolition of old properties and the deepening of the channel. Captain William Galloway, who lived at 3 East Hermitage Place, Leith took up the post of harbourmaster at a salary of £150 per annum on 1st July. One condition of his employment was that he would not take part in the affairs of the town council, thus limiting his duties:

1. To see that all ships arriving are properly moored and berthed.
2. To see that proper arrangements are made for the discharge of ships' ballast expeditiously and to arrange the judicious depositing of same.
3. To see that no unnecessary delay takes place in the loading or unloading of cargoes.
4. To regulate the work of pilots.

By the beginning of June, the council accepted the agreement reached over the rails, with the company agreeing to pay and have rights (though not exclusive) to operate over them. The town council would arrange to lay the rails and lease land to the NBR at £15 per annum to build a goods shed. John Walker, General Manager of the North British, declared that there would be no requirement for the three steelyards to weigh the wagons entering the harbour as they expected to be the sole users of the dock and all coal would be weighed at Thornton.

At the same time as its confrontation with the town council, the North British was trying to purchase the Crown rights to a necessary section of the foreshore by the harbour. The Assistant Secretary to the Board of Trade, C. Cecil Trevor, responded to the company's request to make the purchase by pointing out that the North British Railway (No. 3) (Burntisland Dock) Bill, then passing through Parliament, would be opposed if the position was not resolved. By March, the Board of Trade offered the rights to two acres 17 perches of the foreshore at a cost of £150.

However, progress remained slow and by the middle of August, Meik intimated to George Wieland that the works remaining before the dock could open included the erection of the hoists and the laying of the crucial rails. Meik strongly recommended against threatening Armstrong, the contractor, with penalties as this had resulted in work being stopped completely in the past. Instead, Meik wrote to Armstrong intimating the NBR's wish to see the work completed by the winter of 1876 and that the erection of the hoists was alone in his contract in holding up the completion. He believed that the work could be expedited and asked to meet the Directors of Armstrong's to hasten the fulfilment of the contract. In addition, he urged Scott to do everything his foreman, Mr Fairbairn, required to complete the masonry. Eventually, the dock was completed within the revised timetable and made ready for shipping.

The opening of the West Dock was a very grand occasion in the life of the Burgh of Burntisland. As was deemed appropriate, the usual pomp and ceremony attended the day, but in addition, there were one or two minor misfortunes! The shops in town closed for a half-day holiday at midday on 1st December, 1876, the population gathering to witness a great assembly. This included coalmasters from all over Fife, having arrived on several trains from the North, while other guests crossed the Forth by ferry from Granton. As the ferries arrived in Burntisland, the passengers marvelled at every ship dressed overall. Civic dignitaries and a local band marched to the PS *Express*, which had recently been retired from the Tay crossing, and which was moored at the East passenger pier where the Directors of the company welcomed them aboard. The winter weather was turning stormy, as the Forth has a habit of doing, but undaunted, the captain of the steamer set out for the new dock, braving the choppy waters of the Firth.

As the *Express* turned into the new dock gates, the first disaster befell the vessel as her offside paddle became attached to the chain of a lighter that was moored at the entrance. As the *Express* began to drift towards the new breakwater, consternation broke out amongst the dignitaries on board. After half an hour delay, during which time men were sent to clear the paddle, the boat was ready to make a second attempt to enter the dock with the time now at 1.10 pm. On the second attempt, the captain was successful and the vessel cut the ribbon across the entrance to great cheering and no doubt much relief!

The Chairman of the Burntisland Harbour Commission, Provost James Robertson, made a short speech declaring the dock open and the hydraulic lifts immediately began to load the waiting ships, accompanied by a salute from the battery at Rossend Castle, nearby. The hoists were the first of their kind in Scotland and so attracted much interest. One of the two in use at the opening had raised four wagons and successfully tipped the coals into the hold of the waiting ship below. However, the mishaps were not over for the day as the fifth wagon did not tip towards the quayside, but reversed and emptied its full load towards the spectators beneath. Contemporary reports do not reveal any

Coal wagons awaiting loading at the West dock before the viaduct and line to Edinburgh were built.   *Kirkcaldy Museum/418.10*

Hydraulic accumulator (or Power House) at the West dock.   *James F. McEwan/N3295*

injuries amongst those witnessing the event, so it must be assumed that no one was seriously hurt.

As it was, the PS *Express* then took its party back to the passenger pier where they landed without further incident at 2.00 pm. The formal part of the day now over, celebrations continued with 135 gentlemen of the district sitting down to cake and wine, followed by speeches from Provost Robertson, Provost Swan of Kirkcaldy, Harrison for the NBR and Landale for the coalmasters. Dinner was later served at 5.00 pm.in the Forth Hotel for a more select group of 59 guests.

The docks were considered the most modern of their kind and the builders proudly revealed some statistics about the work undertaken and the facilities provided. Visitors were able to see the magnificent new hydraulic machinery including an engine, boiler and tank house, erected a few yards north of the pier. The smooth motion resulted from hydraulic power, installed by Armstrong, and which was considered by Meik to be superior to steam. The wagons were not 'strained' he reported and 'coal breakages kept to a minimum'. Attached to the engine house was a wooden building about 50 feet high and 12 feet square, which was, called the accumulator. It contained a water cylinder, pressurised to 72 tons, the pressure being raised by a 16 horse power engine. The hydraulics then conveyed the water in underground pipes three inches in diameter (nearer to the accumulator, it was four inches) to the two large hoists on the opposite side of the dock at a pressure, maintained at approximately 800 lb. per square inch. All the machinery for the hoists was positioned underground.

The hoists were on a strong wooden frame 30 feet high and could raise 14 tons in one lift. Up to 1,000 tons of coal could thus be dispatched daily, a vast improvement on previous facilities. Only two of the four planned hoists were constructed initially, but this permitted over 200 wagons to be handled daily. The dock gates were also hydraulically operated, by equipment beneath the dock masonry. Provision was made to open and close the gates in an emergency by means of a capstan and diagonally projecting levers, which were also underground. The gates across the 39 ft 6 in. entrance were mitred, swung on large hinges and when closed formed a bridge from one side of the dock to the other. Messrs Turnbull and Oliver produced the mooring palls and ladders along the quayside, which totalled 1,860 feet. Lighting was provided by 27 gas lamps around the dockside, while the provision of all wood and carpentry was contracted to a local joiner, George Ferguson.

The dock was now 5½ acres in area, 30 feet deep and could accommodate four moderately sized ships. The walls were constructed of ashlar sandstone blocks, 12 feet at the base and four feet at the top all on a bed of concrete or, in places, piles. Walter Scott and Company, the contractor, like Armstrong came from Newcastle and was responsible for deepening the channel at the entrance to the new dock and for the foundations of the hoists. At the opening, not all of the work had been completed, for although the old Ironcraig pier had been removed, there were still rails to be laid. The work was done in due course.

The citizens of Burntisland were less protective of the harbour than were their representatives on either the town council or the harbour committee. While

Hand tinted print of the West dock from above Harbour Place and the line to Inverkeithing.
Douglas Yuill Collection

Coal hoist No.2, West dock Burntisland (with mysteriously missing rails!).
Douglas Yuill Collection

complaining that the facilities at the port were inadequate, the electorate still wanted to put the NBR in charge. It may even have seemed that they would be glad to lose all responsibility for the enterprise, for in the local elections of 1880 it was reported that the voters were in favour of transferring liability for the docks to the North British. An amicable agreement was, however, reached over the sale of the gas works, build by the E&NR to serve the terminal and pier at Burntisland. It was sold to Burntisland town council for £5,900 along with five workmen's cottages in Gas Works Terrace and small garden area for another £400.

Traffic at the new dock was affected in 1877 by a 15-week lockout of miners in Fife and Clackmannan. A dispute had arisen over the coal masters' imposition of a 10 per cent cut in wages due to the fall in demand for coal, only six months after the report that further pits were being sunk to meet increasing demand. Regular meetings of the coalowners' association were held in Burntisland throughout the summer and a resolution was worked out in August 1877. Discussions dragged on for several weeks afterwards.

The feuding between the NBR and the town council did not end with the opening of the West dock. Shortage of space at the harbour soon became the next controversial issue. On 2nd May, 1878, the NB received a letter from the Fife Coal Company asking for siding space for 65 wagons, illustrating the demands that the coalmasters were placing on the company for space to handle their traffic. The council added to the company's troubles by levying an additional rate of one penny per ton to use the hoists and other coal handling machinery within the confines of the harbour.

The dispute had to be resolved quickly and so went to arbitration rather than be allowed to drag on. Sir Henry Tyler, MP, an arbitrator appointed by the Board of Trade, on Saturday 15th May, 1880, heard preliminaries of proceedings brought by the railway company against the magistrates and town council as harbour trustees. Additionally, the North British believed that it was wrong to insist that the coal traders were responsible for haulage of their wagons over the rails within the harbour.

Sir Henry had sat in arbitration over a previous dispute between the two parties in 1878 when the liabilities of the NBR over the now notorious quayside rails were considered. Then the NBR had arranged with the coal traders that it would keep the rates uniform at Burntisland and Charlestown. However, the company owned the port at Charlestown but was merely part trustee at Burntisland. This meant that it had control over the track to the quayside at its own port but had to yield to the harbour trustees' arrangements at Burntisland. The council said that the NBR should take the wagons from the pits to the quayside at Burntisland for the rate of 1s. 6d. per ton, the company maintaining that it was only responsible for transport to the boundary of the harbour trustees' property as agreed in 1876. To work beyond the boundary, the North British required an additional 1½d. per ton. The trustees agree to this initially, but when the NBR asked for 2d. per ton, the trustees proposed that they should seek an alternative carrier to handle the traders' wagons.

Prior to the West dock opening, the traders had horses of their own and used them to haul wagons within the dock. The NBR had initially worked the wagons without

West dock Burntisland in pre-Grouping days.   *Douglas Yuill Collection*

Passenger ferry slipway at the West dock, with gable of waiting room centre.
James F. McEwan/N3323

charge, and included that part of the rate within the overall tariff from the colliery to the ship. Sir Henry Tyler had arbitrated in 1878 that the North British was not bound to provide the additional service and that its obligation ceased at the end of the NBR system, namely the entrance to Burntisland docks. Indeed, he found that the NBR had no powers to levy a rate for work within the harbour. The trustees did not have such powers either and so Tyler found that the traders should pay for the internal haulage.

A report on traffic through the dock was submitted weekly to North British headquarters and snapshot of the shipping loaded at Burntisland can be seen from those in 1883, sent by Stewart, the district superintendent, to John Walker. Extracts from these reports reveal the seasonal nature of the trade.

Week ending	steamers	tons	sailing vessels	tons	total tons
23rd January	8	6,019	3	728	6,747
26th March	13	12,025	6	1,928	13,953
28th May	13	14,809	9	2,224	17,033
23rd July	5	5,671	4	1,035	6,706
24th September	8	7,736	9	2,739	10,475
26th November	14	15,399	3	536	15,935

During the same period, the imports were few and consisted mainly of esparto grass for paper making, straw, flax, maize, linseed, and sleepers.

By the mid-1880s, the fight with Methil was developing and on 7th September, 1886 the NBR senior management sought a target of 25,000 tons of coal per week at Burntisland. This was immediately reached the following week, when 25,937 tons were loaded into 33 vessels, 19 of them steamers.

Randolph Wemyss had secured what was, in effect, a monopoly of the traffic from the eastern end of the Fife coalfields both from his own pits and from those of the Fife Coal Company in the district. However, the coal proprietors of the West Fife coalfield soon found the advantages of using Burntisland to export their output. Some used both Methil and Burntisland and many of these were listed in *Slater's Directory* of 1893:

Dunfermline	Henry Ness & Company	Townhill
	John Nimmo & Son	Rosebank
	Thomas Spowart & Company Ltd.	Lassodie
	Townhill Coal Company	Townhill
	Wallace Brothers	Kingseat
Cowdenbeath	Blairadam Coal Company	Kelty
	Cowdenbeath Coal Company	Cowdenbeath
	Fife Coal Company	Cowdenbeath
Lochgelly	Lochgelly Iron and Coal Company	Lochgelly
	Lochore & Capeldrae Cannel Coal Company	Lochore
Cardenden	Dundonald Coal Company	Cardenden
	Denend Coal Company	Cardenden

Within Burntisland, only two coal traders were listed in the North British Trader's wagon register. These were Robert Lawson and Archibald Smith, both coal merchants in the town.

PS *John Stirling* tied up along the western quayside at Burntisland.

Kirkcaldy Museum/1982.143

PS *William Muir* arriving at the New pier at Burntisland in NBR days following modifications.

Kirkcaldy Museum/289.9

New Boats

In 1874, the company became concerned about the condition of its boats and ordered reports from Board of Trade surveyors on the condition of PS *Thane of Fife*, PS *Express*, PS *Auld Reekie* and PS *Forth*. Replacements for the *Express* and *Forth* were set on the ferry crossing at the end of the 1870s. Responsibility for the procurement of the boats was delegated to William Muir, and he reported to the Board on 4th February, 1875 that he had concluded a contract with John Key of Abden shipyard at Kinghorn for two new passenger steamers at a cost of £17,750. The contract was signed by Muir and fellow Director John Beaumont in August 1875. Both boats were named after company Directors and were intended to handle the additional traffic which would be brought by the new Tay Bridge when it opened. The first to enter service was PS *John Stirling* in 1876 followed in 1879 by a boat that was to become most closely associated with the crossing for the following 57 years, the PS *William Muir*.

However, the North British was not happy with the vessel at first and instituted an action against the builders for £1,000. On 6th November, 1879, the NBR lodged the claim against Key for the late delivery of *William Muir* and 'her failure to perform on the Granton to Burntisland passage, pier to pier, in the time specified'.

The *John Stirling* was powered by a two cylinder simple engine, also built by John Key at the company's Whitebank engine works at Heggie's Wynd in Kirkcaldy. She ran on the Burntisland route until the Forth Bridge was opened and was subsequently sold in 1892. The *John Stirling* was involved in an incident in the Forth on 7th October, 1879 when the trawler *Integrity* was sunk following a collision with the ferry in thick fog. A claim was brought against the NBR by the owners of the trawler, Lord Rutherford Clark finding against the North British and awarding the trawler's owner £870 plus costs.

Despite her earlier failure to live up to the company's expectations, the *William Muir* was admired by her regular passengers, and entered the hearts of many Fifers. She remained on the route almost continuously until 1937. At 364 tons, she was lighter than her sister (the *John Stirling* was 427 tons), but could carry 950 passengers. Her fate was more certain when the NBR decided to retain her on the Granton to Burntisland crossing after the bulk of the traffic was diverted to the Forth Bridge. Although a slower service, dependent of the state of the river, she provided a valuable service for the locals of Burntisland and visitors alike. On one night, in the autumn of 1889, she ferried the entire George Sanger's circus over the Forth with PS *John Beaumont*, including 50 caravans, 500 horses and many other animals between the hours of 10.00 pm and 4.00 am!

Cruising was a favourite pastime on the Forth both during pleasant summer evenings and as part of a well-earned holiday. Many working people from Edinburgh took to the choppy waters of the firth to enjoy the bracing air, a complete change from the smoky atmosphere of 'Auld Reekie', as the capital was known. However, the NBR was not well disposed to excursionists using the harbour at Burntisland and an application by the Forth River Steam Shipping Company to sail from Burntisland at a rate of 1s. 3d. per trip was refused by the Board.

The North British Steam Packet Company, part of the NBR which controlled the company's coastal steamers, obtained a majority holding in Galloway Saloon Steam Packet Company of Leith in 1889 which was engaged in pleasure cruising on the Firth of Forth. Galloway had previously been marine tonnage contractors trading under the name of MacGregor and Galloway and had been established at Leith since 1856. Galloway was one of the popular carriers, to such an extent that the NBR complained that Galloway's boats interfered with its traffic, and so a substantial shareholding was one way of containing the competition. Galloway's fleet was to provide relief boats for the *William Muir* in the future.

The Kirkcaldy and District Railway

The North British continued to seek ways of shortening the route from the West Fife coalfield to Burntisland, to win over more of the traffic from the coalmasters who might be tempted to use the Wemyss system and Methil docks. A direct route to Burntisland had been ruled out, partly because of the ridge of hills between the port and the inland coal measures and partly because of the opposition from the coal masters. However, rather than continue with the line to Thornton, a suitable (shorter) line was possible from Cowdenbeath through the village of Auchtertool to the coast, south-west of Kirkcaldy. Here there had been a number of attempts to build a railway at Seafield associated with grander schemes to make Kirkcaldy into a coal exporting port to rival both Methil and Burntisland.

What followed was a series of plans and counter-plans from a number of promoters, none of which ended in success. At first, these ideas were initiated with the support of the Caledonian Railway and were incorporated into a Bill for the Alloa, Dunfermline & Kirkcaldy Railway in 1883. An alternative proposal, in part supported by the citizens of Kirkcaldy, the Seafield Dock and Railway Company defeated this measure in Parliament and received an Act in the same year. It had an authorised share capital of £300,000, and was allowed five years for construction and additional works. Amongst these works were a five acre dock at Seafield and six hoists to handle over a million tons of coal annually.

Yet another Act of 1888 allowed an extension of three years for construction and changed the name of the company to the Kirkcaldy and District Railway Company (K&DR). The project was not begun until February 1889 but by September had been suspended. Another Act dated 4th August, 1890 sought an expansion of the works and the authority to raise the capital to pay for the completion of the project. This Act was for a number of mineral lines around Kirkcaldy, Cowdenbeath and Auchterderran, to provide access to new pits, which were being sunk.

Shares for the additional works were not issued by the following year when the time allowed for construction had elapsed and so another Act was authorised on 5th August, 1891. This Act, among a great deal of tidying up of badly-drafted earlier Acts, permitted the Kirkcaldy and District Railway to carry passengers which had been expressly prohibited under previous legislation. Once more, the shadow of the Caledonian Railway was cast over the proposal, more seriously with the intention of shipping coal to the West, away from the Fife ports, by supporting an alternative scheme. Had this been successful, the traffic at Burntisland (and Methil) might have been adversely affected.

When the North British Railway entered the scene in 1894, partly in an effort to prevent the K&DR falling into the hands of the Caley, it sought to dissolve the K&DR and transfer the undertaking to the NBR. The latest Act, given Royal Assent on 6th July, 1895, permitted a siding from the Burntisland to Kirkcaldy route to the shore at Seafield and various other colliery lines adjacent to the Dunfermline branch. The drift mine at Seafield, operated by the Fife Coal Company between 1920 and 1939, was the remnant of the earlier proposals for the area. In the 1930s, sand was also taken from the foreshore and taken via Invertiel sidings to the main line. The siding was closed with the development of a new Seafield colliery in the 1950s.

The through route to Auchtertool and Cowdenbeath was completed by the NBR and the 7 mile 26 chain line was opened on a wintry Tuesday 3rd March, 1896. The opening was reported both in the *Fifeshire Advertiser* and the *Fife Free Press*, which carried the following report on Saturday 7th March, revealing more about the origins of the line.

The Kirkcaldy and District railway, from Kirkcaldy to Foulford Junction, near Cowdenbeath, was formally opened for traffic on Tuesday. The line, which was inspected a week ago on behalf of the Board of Trade, and passed the necessary requirements, is a single line of rails branching off the main line at Invertiel Junction, about a mile to the west of Kirkcaldy station. From that point, it traverses a distance of six miles to Foulford Junction, where it joins the Dunfermline line. On the route, the railway taps various small villages, the principal being Auchtertool, where a station is planned, and a Station Master has been appointed to look after the interests of the company. The railway was first formulated in connection with the now defunct Seafield Dock Scheme some years ago by the Kirkcaldy and District Railway Company. An attempt was made some years ago in Parliament, in an indirect way to obtain an opening into Fife for the Caledonian Railway Company by means of a new route, but the North British defeated any attempt in this direction by taking over the new railway and making an offer to contribute £150,000 or half whatever sum would be expended in the construction of new harbour and docks for Kirkcaldy. The new railway will be utilised principally for coal traffic via the Raith sidings to Burntisland dock and three trains will be run daily from 7.00 am. to 5.00 pm.

The first train consisted of a locomotive and inspection saloon and included among the passengers were three inspectors and Mr Lawson, the station master from Kirkcaldy. In a heavy snowfall, the train ran from Invertiel to Cowdenbeath and back, examining (probably with some difficulty) the points and signals *en route*. The station at Auchtertool was on the eastern outskirts of the village and was never more than a goods depot with the only crossing loop on the line. A signal box opened at Auchtertool at the same time as the rest of the line to work the loop and small yard. A letter to the *Fifeshire Advertiser* during the week following the opening revealed the optimism of local people in their desire to see a passenger service introduced: 'Now that there is a railway station and a station master at Auchtertool, we hope that the railway company will soon see their way to open the line for passenger traffic. The historic village of Auchtertool has a charming position and if only it were placed within convenient reach by rail, it would soon become one of the most important resorts in Fife. Even a morning and an evening train would be an immense boon.'

The Board of Trade had insisted on the inclusion of a clause in the 1895 Act to require the NBR to operate passenger services if requested. However, scheduled passenger trains never did run on the line, which throughout its life satisfied its original purpose of shortening the route to Burntisland. The only passenger traffic is likely to have been diversions during work on the main lines or, during World War I, troop trains. This was in part due to the sharp curves, particularly at either end, which would have an adverse effect on passenger stock.

The delivery of coal and agricultural material was the most significant traffic that Auchtertool station could expect, although the nearby distillery was an important customer. There was also a domestic coal merchant established in the early years of the 20th century, Alexander Clark, who rented premises from the North British before World War I. Coal traffic was the main flow, running from west to east to join the main line and gaining access to Burntisland docks from Burntisland East. Return traffic would be empty coal wagons to the collieries of West Fife, sometimes on the direct line, but more often by way of Inverkeithing and round the rest of the circular route to the West Fife coalfield.

The 1896 Rail Accident

A rail accident occurred at Burntisland at the end of 1896, which was contributed to by the complex movement of coal trains to and from the West Fife coalfield on the new direct line. On 9th December, the 4.05 pm up passenger train from Dundee to Edinburgh was headed by Wheatley 2-4-0 No. 424, built in 1873 and fitted with Westinghouse brake. Holmes had rebuilt the whole class of these engines in 1890/1 with improvements such as larger cylinders and a round top cab. There were nine carriages and vans in the afternoon train, that cold December day, as it approached Burntisland at 5.56 pm.

Signalman Sydney Hoskiss at Burntisland East cabin was having a busy time when the passenger train was offered to him by William Birrell, at Kinghorn cabin. A twice-daily trip train had left Burntisland at 8.35 am that morning and was returning from its second visit to the recently opened Auchtertool line. It was not an unusually long train, comprising 17 NBR coal wagons, two private trader wagons, three goods wagons and NBR brake van No. 472. There was no access for it to Burntisland harbour lines due to the congestion on the east side of the station. In addition the 5.35 pm empty mineral train was in the yard, waiting to leave by the down line for Kelty.

The train from the Auchtertool line had been on the up main line at Burntisland Junction cabin for about seven or eight minutes waiting to enter the harbour to discharge at the dock. Robert Paxton, the driver, was then called back by Hoskiss and his guard, James McRae, to Burntisland East in order to enter the harbour by way of the yard. The train came to a stand opposite the cabin, when Hoskiss asked him to take his train further back as he was fouling the east crossing and the Kelty train was waiting to leave. This train would normally have run to Kelty via Dunfermline, but that departure movement would have required the train to be hauled out onto the up line and then stand while the locomotive was run round to the front. Clearly, with the build up of traffic, this was no longer possible and the alternative was to take the train via Thornton Junction.

Hoskiss, when offered the passenger, had forgotten that the Auchtertool branch trip train was still on the up line and accepted it. A collision became inevitable. Locomotive and tender of the passenger train both left the rails, and although the train divided, all the carriages remained on the track, despite suffering damage to six of them. The mineral train did not fare so well. The brake van was demolished and nine wagons were severely damaged, the first six being derailed. Injuries were relatively light, 20 passengers and the guard on the Dundee train were hurt, the latter badly, but no injury was recorded to those on the mineral train.

Although Hoskiss was considered to be at fault for the accident, the 'very loose system' of controlling the trains by the signalmen and yard foremen was criticised by the inspecting officer, Major F.A. Marindin. The yard foreman at the time of the collision was dismissed from the NBR's service for his part in the mishandling of the trains. The 'very loose system' may have improved but was to contribute to the worst accident at Burntisland in 1914, told in full in Chapter Six.

The appendix to the NBR working timetables for 1901 gives the following whistle codes for the two cabins at Burntisland. Drivers would use these to indicate to the signalman which route he wished to take. The table shows the potential number of movements at each cabin.

Burntisland East		*Burntisland Junction*	
Main line, Up or Down	1	Main line, Up or Down	1
To or from goods yard	2	To or from Dock lines	2
To cross from Up to Down line		To cross from Up to Down line or vice versa	3
or vice versa on east crossover	3	From Dock lines towards engine shed	
To cross from Up to Down line		or vice versa	4
or vice versa on west crossover	4	To or from No.1 Dock platform	5
From Up line to Old Dock lines		To or from No.2 Dock platform	6
or vice versa.	5	To or from No.3 Dock platform	7
From Down line to Old Dock lines	6	Dock line to locomotive coal sidings	
			1 long and 1 short
From engine shed to siding	7	Dock line to Goods yard	
			1 long and 2 short
To shunt from Goods yard to Up lines			
2 long and 2 short			

Rival Progress

Burntisland's arch-enemy, Captain Randolph G. E. Wemyss, became laird of Wemyss castle in 1879 and set about developing the coal seams in East Fife. Although of generally poor quality, they were nonetheless valuable and so Wemyss sought opportunities to export his coal. When he was a minor, his mother had funded a dock at West Wemyss as early as 1873.

Local entrepreneurs and coal owners, with the intention of improving the port to provide facilities for coal export, established the Leven Harbour Company in 1877. The new Leven docks, which were created with the help of the North British Railway, were constantly subject to silting up and additional investment could not be found to enlarge the harbour further. It was suggested at the time that the NBR had made the raising of capital difficult to avoid competition for its dock at Burntisland.

Unfortunately for both the NBR and Burntisland harbour, the outcome was to produce even more competition for the NBR's port. Captain Wemyss decided to open his first dock at Methil. As part of the improvement, he built the Wemyss and Buckhaven Railway (W&BR) in August 1881 from Thornton Junction, on the main North British main line, to Buckhaven. A short extension at the eastern end of this line would provide the Earl with that element, essential for his success, access from the West Fife coalfield via the NBR to his new port at Methil. To further his plans, Wemyss bought Leven dock in 1883 and undertook to keep it open. At the same time, he negotiated with the main coal owners, Fife Coal Company and Bowman & Co. to handle an agreed proportion of their output through Methil.

The North British opposed the development at Methil but was unsuccessful and the new dock opened in 1887. Having achieved his aim of a convenient port for his (and his neighbour's) coal, Wemyss then went about selling the dock to the North British Railway. The NBR was obliged to agree to the purchase since it could not afford to allow a rival railway company to encroach on its monopoly in Fife. Wemyss realised this and so was able to demand several concessions in the agreement. As part of the purchase, the NBR obtained the W&BR, Leven dock and the associated railways for a total of £225,000. Wemyss undertook not to jeopardise the Methil dock by mining beneath it or by building a competing port to the NBR's other Forth ports at Burntisland and Charlestown, further up river, in addition to Methil. He gained free access to the NBR's newly acquired Muiredge branch nearby, and all other conveyance would be at rates no higher than at Burntisland and Charlestown.

The crowning glory for Captain Randolph Gordon Erskine Wemyss was his appointment as a Director of the North British Railway Company, a position that was to prove to be an irritant to Burntisland. The final blow for Burntisland was the understanding, which Wemyss believed that he had received from John Walker, NBR General Manager, that if Methil needed to be expanded then the North British would undertake the required work. This was indeed the case soon afterwards and by 1891, an Act was obtained to construct a further new dock at Methil. The dock opened in 1901.

Meanwhile, trade continued to grow at Burntisland. During week ending 21st September, 1886 8,218 wagons 'crossed over the steelyards' (were weighed), 1,722 on the 15th alone, a record for the port up to then. The previous highest number of wagons in one day had been 1,517. There were other coal owners in the West Fife area who used Burntisland as their chosen point of export, amongst which were Henry Ness of Townhill, John Nimmo and Son of Rosebank, Wallace of Kingseat and the Blairadam Coal Company. Denend Coal Company and Dundonald Coal Company of Cardenden and the Lochore and Capeldrae Cannel Coal Company from Central Fife also used the port. On the record week, 16,138 tons came from Thornton pits, 7,849 tons from Townhill, 9,979 tons from Kelty and even 3,205 tons from the Alloa area.

The town council sent a deputation to John Walker of the NBR to seek enlargement of the accommodation at Burntisland to cope with the increase in traffic. Although initially unresponsive, Walker knew that Charlestown was quite small and could not handle the levels of coal export which were envisaged. Additionally, Wemyss was pressing for enlargement of his docks but when James Connacher replaced Walker as General Manager, a change of mind was apparent. Connacher was a supporter of the expansion at Burntisland.

East Dock

In order to break the supremacy of the Wemyss system and the harbour facilities at Methil, the NBR became keen to promote the extension of harbour facilities at Burntisland. In so doing, it aimed to encourage the coalmasters of West Fife to use that port exclusively for the shipment of their coal. The NBR wanted to develop this trade because in the early years of coal-mining it was from Lanarkshire and the West of Scotland that coal for the company's locomotives was drawn and the most easily worked seams were already being worked out.

Shipments of coal grew steadily up to the end of the century, reaching just short of one million tons annually in 1900. The same year, the North British Railway boasted that the standage at Burntisland could receive 1,000 wagons. Additionally, it was becoming necessary to accommodate ships of greater tonnage than hitherto since such vessels from the Mediterranean had begun to visit the Forth.

The ownership of the port changed in 1881 when a further Act, the Burntisland Harbour Act (44 & 45 Vict. cap. lxxxv), vested the harbour in commissioners for the improvement and other works. There were to be eight commissioners, four each from the town and the railway company. They were to be appointed within two weeks of the Royal Assent and then elected from November 1881. The North British Railway's further advance of £100,000 was also acknowledged in the Act.

The area which the West dock had created was soon to prove insufficient and, in July 1896 the Royal Assent was given to an Act, (59 & 60 Vict. cap. clv) Burntisland Harbour Act, to provide another deep water dock at Burntisland

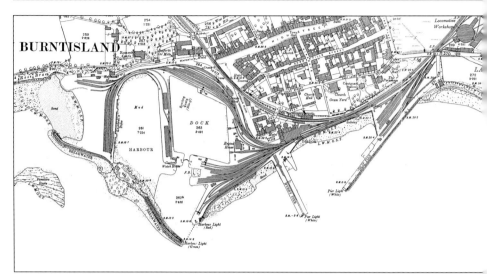

The 1894 Ordnance Survey map showing Burntisland prior to construction of the East dock.
National Library of Scotland

Construction of the East dock at Burntisland around 1901, Burntisland Junction signal cabin to right. *Kirkcaldy Museum 1977/1431*

within seven years. The North British had given authority to Burntisland Harbour Commission to give notice of a Bill and the NBR would raise the capital. The amount involved on this occasion was £300,000.

Again, Thomas Meik and Sons were responsible for the plans. Their engineer, P.W. Meik, was familiar with the docks having previously worked on the West dock. He had also held responsibility as resident engineer on the construction of the Forth Bridge. Tenders were invited and on 19th January, 1897 a contract was signed with Sir John Jackson of Westminster for construction works including a sea wall, two entrance piers and a new ferry pier. A small irony was apparent at this stage, for the contractors were the same as at Methil docks, which were only partially open by then. At the same time as the Act, the composition of the Harbour Commission was altered to nine representatives of the NBR and only three from Burntisland town council, a move which would reduce the tensions between town and company.

Arrangements had to be made to accommodate the movements of Sir John Jackson's locomotive on the harbour system. The *Appendix to the Working Timetables* of 1901, show that the NBR authorised the contractor's light engine to operate over the dock and other lines between the new harbour works at the west breakwater and Lammerlaws siding. However, it was not permitted to foul the main line. All movements had to be under the marshalman's orders. Movements between Burntisland Junction cabin and the new sidings constructed at Lammerlaws for the increased traffic came under the supervision of a pilot guard, although this arrangement was suspended in 1901.

The design for the new dock had a number of aspects to consider before work could commence. Four schemes were submitted to the harbour commissioners, two on sites to the east and two on sites to the west of the existing deep harbour. A site to the east was chosen, originally providing 7½ acres, although this was subsequently increased to 11½ acres. The chosen site gave a shared entrance with the existing dock, but extended seawards and widened, making connection between the two docks possible.

However, the most important point for the North British Railway in the selection of an eastern site was that the vast majority of coal traffic continued to approach the town from the east. Consequently, the rail access could remain the same, but the new dock would sweep away the old passenger ferry pier and so, during construction, a temporary pier was provided outside the cofferdam. The comparisons with the West dock show the contrast in proportions between the old and new.

About 37½ acres were reclaimed from the river, a lengthy operation, which began immediately the contract, was signed. A breakwater was created from material removed from the Lammerlaws, the rocky promontory to the east. The contractor laid down temporary rails and tipping from end- and side-door wagons began in order to create the sea wall. Very fine sand was pumped from a nearby sandbank and transported in barges behind the wall to make it watertight. To speed up this transfer, a mound of sand was deposited alongside the now redundant old goods pier. By March 1899 this was so high that it cut off the area to the east.

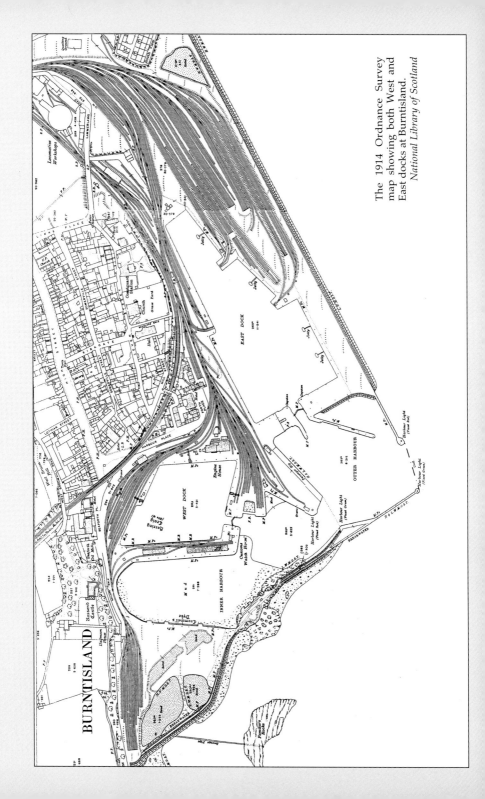

The 1914 Ordnance Survey map showing both West and East docks at Burntisland. *National Library of Scotland*

The new entrance was substantial, being 60 feet wide and provided with both dock and sea gates. The outer or sea gates were intended to be closed when the Forth became too stormy and were constructed of steel by Siemens-Martin. These heavy gates were operated by hydraulic rams. Hoists were erected on the south quayside, established on concrete jetties 59 feet wide. The power for the hoists was supplied from a building adjacent to the original hydraulic pump house and slightly to the west. It contained two boilers to replace the old ones. The new hydraulic pumping engines powered the three hoists each with a 40 ft lift, the dock gates, two accumulators and ancillary capstans and turntables. The quayside added up to a grand 1,965 feet. The dock opened for traffic in August 1901.

Vessels up to 5,000 tons could be accommodated in the new dock. In August 1910, SS *The Indian Monarch* sailed carrying the greatest tonnage dealt with at the port, 5,425 tons of coal destined for Bueneos Aires, plus an additional 1,596 tons of bunker coal. Indeed vessels up to 400 feet long could be loaded from the coal hoists without moving position. The annual exports in 1855 had been 6,000 tons!

The North British Railway sidings occupied about 18 acres on three sides and amounted to 4½ miles of track with direct access from the main line totalling five furlongs. A degree of gravity feed and return was incorporated in the layout of the sidings to speed up movement within the dock. The hoist on the north side had a high level return facility for returning empty wagons whereas those on the south side of the dock had to return the wagons to ground level first. On the high level hoist, the wagons left on a curve with a radius of 80 feet and a sharp gradient of 1 in 30 easing to 1 in 90. To accommodate the wheels, the gauge on the curve was relaxed to 4 ft 9¼ in. and superelevated slightly. The approach sidings to the north hoist were at 1 in 120, while those on the two southern ones were 1 in 90 round the five chain radius curves. All three hoists lifted wagons 40 feet above the quayside and were capable of delivering 2,000 tons in a 10-hour working day. The hoists in the West dock could handle 1,000 tons per working day.

With all the hoists working in both docks, over 60,000 tons of coal could be shipped in one week. The greatest amount handled by 1912 was 68,100 tons which is the equivalent of 11,350 tons per working day. In one hour, as many as 60 wagons could be dealt with at one of the high level hoists, equal to 480 tons. An anti-breakage device was fitted to one of the hoists and was well received by the shippers. It was invented by a railwayman in order to reduce the damage, which could be suffered by the coal being loaded by a conventional chute.

Between the entrances to the West and East docks, a new ferry pier was constructed with a landing slip gradient which varied between 1 in 15 and 1 in 30, and which was paved throughout its length. A large quantity of whinstone was blasted away to permit the ferry to approach at low tide. Thomas Meik along with Robert Henderson superintended the work, Henderson acting as resident engineer for the Harbour Commissioners.

The Earl of Wemyss was not happy at the amount of money that the NBR had spent on Burntisland, believing that this left less for Methil, prejudicing the growth of the East Fife coalfield. What angered him most was the understanding that he thought he had to develop Methil when trade required it, at the NBR's expense, discussion over which the NBR Directors refused to countenance.

The coal chute at the East Dock in 1937, with two rakes of mineral wagons waiting loading of bauxite in the distance.
St Andrews University Library/JV A5373

Coal hoist No. 6 at the East dock in the 1930s. *Edward Wilson Collection*

The North British had kept faith with Burntisland and so expected a commitment from the coal owners of West Fife to use the port. In 1898, a new agreement was reached between the company and 28 of West Fife coalmasters. All the following companies and individuals had agreed to support the need for the new deep-water dock at Burntisland:

Cowdenbeath Coal Company	Cowdenbeath
Lochgelly Iron and Coal Company	Lochgelly
Fife Coal Company	Townhill, Dunfermline
Wemyss Coal Company	West Wemyss
Randolph Erskine Wemyss	Wemyss and Torry
Thomas Spowart and Company	Lassodie, Dunfermline
Donibristle Colliery Company	Donibristle, Crossgates (James Armstrong Nasmyth)
Bowman and Company	Buckhaven (David Cairns)
Archibald Bowman	Buckhaven
Robert Cairns, Shipping Agent	Leith
Wallace Brothers	Halbeath (Robert Walker Wallace)

In return, the coalmasters agreed to confine all their shipments from Fife to ports from time to time served by the NBR for 21 years from the end of December 1895. Additionally, they resolved to ship coal only from a port in Fife served by the NBR and would send their own traffic or any other solely by NBR lines. The coalmasters were also prevented by the agreement from promoting or constructing any new line in Fife, except a private siding approved by the NBR. However, a final clause continued to exempt Randolph Wemyss and the Wemyss Coal Company who were permitted to consign their coal from West Wemyss harbour and to build new railways to connect their pits to the docks at Methil.

Wemyss lost no time in planning his own private railway and the North British could do little to prevent the entrepreneurial earl from building and operating it himself. He resigned his Directorship in 1899 having achieved all he wanted from the hapless NBR. His new railway was opened in 1901.

Cowdenbeath Collieries Company wagon.   *HMRS/APC026*

Lochgelly Iron and Coal Company wagon.   *HMRS/W371*

Donibristle Colliery Company wagon.   *Author's Collection*

Sketch plan of Donibristle Colliery and the direct connection to Seafield dock.

Author's Collection

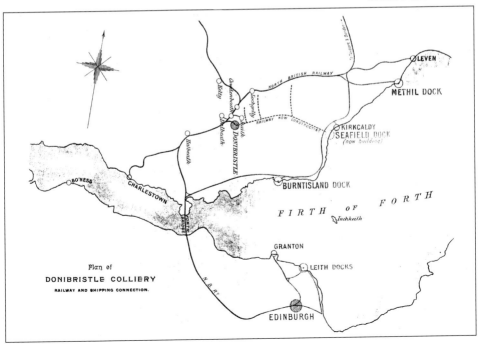

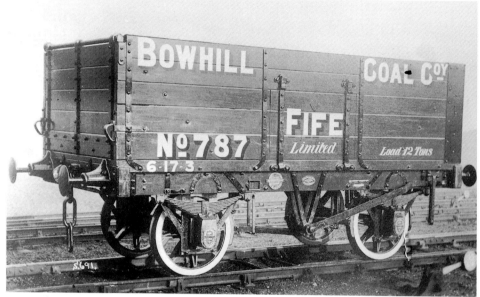

Bowhill Coal Company wagon.   *HMRS/T15-2*

Dundonald Coal Company wagon.   *HMRS/T16-18*

The agreements reached with the coalmasters did not preclude them complaining about the rates that they were being charged. On 24th January, 1895, the Donibristle Colliery Company wrote to the Board of Trade to complain about 'the unfair rates for coal and dross'. These had risen from 3s. 2d. and 3s. 6d. respectively in December 1892 to 4s. 2d. and 4s. 6d. in 1894. However, their complaint tells us more about the destination for their output, which was sent to Bervie and Johnshaven, Aberfoyle and Drymen, Dunbar and Berwick, Galashiels and Kelso and Longforgan and Blairgowrie amongst many other places.

The *Fife Free Press* of 8th December, 1894 stated, 'Harbour Trade Burntisland. Board of Trade returns for November show that the shipment of coal for November is gradually returning to about its normal extent. During the past month 61 steamers and 17 sailing vessels cleared outwards with cargo, the total coal shipments amounted to 60,955 tons as against 63,891 for the corresponding month last year. The import trade was fairly steady'.

The tonnage exported from Burntisland continued to grow at the end of the 19th century, rising by more than 50 per cent between 1898 and 1902 (from 827,743 tons to 1,294,173 tons). The greatest volume was exported to Germany, with Sweden receiving similar quantities of around 450,000 tons per annum. Comparison of tonnages exported through Methil with those exported through Burntisland show the rise of its neighbour and the constant pressure for the NBR to counter the drift to the east in order to retain its traffic.

	Burntisland tons	Methil tons	
1877	288,919	40,000	(approximately)
1887	724,402	219,884	
1897	886,935	1,090,324	
1902	1,524,207	1,759,041	
1906	2,013,454	2,793,257	

However, Methil was clearly winning the battle, as Burntisland's percentage of the county's output rose from 22 per cent in 1877 to 29 per cent in 1887 but fell back to 21 per cent in 1897. That many of the coal owners remained faithful to Burntisland, despite the dispute over the rates to be charged, was seen from evidence, which was presented to Parliament during the passage of the Buckhaven Dock bill of 1907. During the year ended January 1905, the following coal owners exported the majority of their output through Burntisland.

Coal Owner	Location	Methil tons	Burntisland
Bowhill Coal Company,	Cardenden	91,541	118,514
Coltness Iron Company	Blairhall	5,041	8,925
Dundonald Collieries	Cardenden	12,767	16,246
Donibristle Coal Company	Cowdenbeath	12,237	27,857
Lochgelly Iron & Coal Co.	Lochgelly	8,512	475,939
Thomas Spowart & Co.	Kelty	22,143	70,886

Only Fife Coal Company amongst the major coal owners exported more through Methil, although this was due to the high proportion of its output being produced by those of its pits in the East Fife district.

THE NORTH BRITISH RAILWAY AND ITS CONNECTIONS IN CENTRAL SCOTLAND.

Map of the North British Railway in 1904.

Chapter Six

The Twentieth Century

Disagreements with the coal masters dragged on into the 20th century, almost entirely revolving round the rate of carriage of coals and the use of the harbour lines. The Burntisland agreement of 1896 was invoked whereby the North British undertook to maintain the relative position amongst all its Forth ports, Methil, Grangemouth, Bo'ness, Charlestown, and Burntisland. In 1908, the NBR increased the dues payable by shipping berthed at Methil, and the Burntisland harbour commissioners did the same at Burntisland, but failed to decrease the charges made for trimming the loads, which had been applied at Bo'ness and Grangemouth. Further conflict was to follow.

Burntisland town council was still suspicious of the actions of the NBR into the 20th century and under the leadership of Provost John Connel, Managing Director of the Lochgelly Iron and Coal Company, started to take a stronger line with the company. However, Connel, in his last act before retirement, weakened in his resolve and used his casting vote in a split council to accept crippling loans from the North British. The interest repayments were so high that the burgh could ill afford them. The relationship with the NBR was the main election issue and a celebrated local citizen, James Lothian Mitchell, who was successfully elected to the council in 1903, took part in the fight.

Mitchell, on election found himself set against the Dean of Guild, Archibald Stocks. Stocks and Connel feared exposure by Mitchell for the alleged incompetence of their dealings with the railway company. Stocks had a cosy relationship having formerly worked at the Roundhouse, although he had become a publican in Burntisland after leaving the railway's employment. On becoming a town councillor, Mitchell's support grew and the council's dealings with the NBR took a colder turn. A radical and champion of the working man, James Mitchell was popular with his voters but not so with local businesses, not the least the NBR. In taking on the railway, he was declaring himself against corruption in burgh affairs.

The Lochgelly Iron and Coal Company subsequently brought an action over the company's charges against both the railway and the harbour commission, the matter remaining unresolved until 1913, when the House of Lords found in favour of the coalmasters. By that time only Fife Coal Company, Wemyss Coal Company and Thomas Spowart remained to share the Lochgelly Iron and Coal Company's success. The new charges were applied to all companies including those in the recently formed Fife and Clackmannan Coal Owners Association, but any reduction before 1922 at Grangemouth or Bo'ness would apply to Methil and Burntisland. The NBR agreed to pay the coal masters £47,500 in settlement of their claims against the company.

A new class of locomotive appeared at Burntisland shed in 1909, when two examples of Reid's class 'A' 0-6-2Ts (LNER 'N15') were sent to the port from new. As goods engines, Nos. 861 and 862 were intended to haul the coal traffic and were put to use on the Auchtertool branch and replaced the Holmes 0-6-0Ts

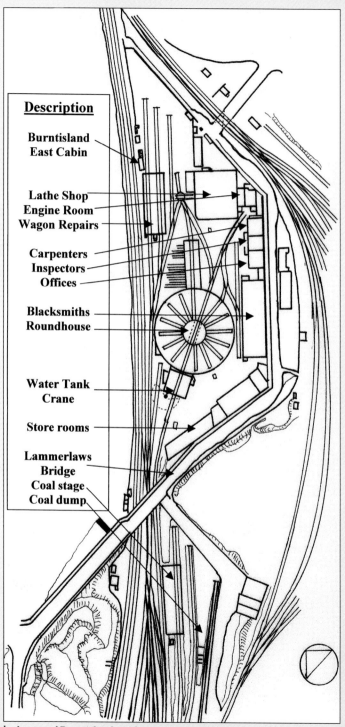

Description

Burntisland
East Cabin

Lathe Shop
Engine Room
Wagon Repairs

Carpenters
Inspectors
Offices

Blacksmiths
Roundhouse

Water Tank
Crane

Store rooms

Lammerlaws
Bridge
Coal stage
Coal dump

Sketch of the layout of Burntisland works.

Author

(LNER class 'J83'). As most of the class had been sent to operate the Cowlairs incline, successfully replacing the long-standing rope haulage, it was not long before the Fife pair joined them at Eastfield. NBR class 'G' 0-4-0STs (LNER 'Y9') also operated in the dock area of Burntisland.

As the 20th century opened, traffic settled down with Burntisland now one of many stations on the main line. Passenger fares to various parts of Scotland were published in the North British Timetables for June 1900.

		Single		Return	
		s.	d.	s.	d.
Aberdeen	1st	19	0	31	6
	3rd	9	0	15	0
Dundee	1st	6	6	11	0
	3rd	3	5 ½	6	11
Edinburgh	1st	2	6	4	0
	3rd	1	0	2	0
Glasgow	1st	7	2	11	6
	3rd	3	3	5	3
Stirling	1st	5	6	8	6
	3rd	2	3 ½	5	5

Passenger services were 'increased and improved' by the NBR when, in the summer of 1900, it promoted the attractions of the Fife coast to commuters. Businessmen, who took summer homes for the family while they travelled daily to Edinburgh, were offered fortnightly and monthly season tickets at moderate rates. The advertised trains from the East Neuk (commencing at St Andrews, Crail or Leven) departed from Burntisland at 7.31 am and 8.15 am for arrival at Waverley and at 7.38 am for Glasgow Queen Street. Return departures were at 4.50 pm and 4.55 pm from Waverley and 4.07 pm or 5.35pm from Queen Street. The 4.07 pm train met the Edinburgh service at Dalmeny before running on to Dunfermline Upper. The arrivals at Burntisland were 5.30 pm, 5.48 pm and 6.52 pm.

The first down train of the day was a workmen's service from Dunfermline Upper at 6.07 am, which travelled via Inverkeithing north and east junctions to Ladybank, calling at Burntisland at 6.39 am. This train was followed by the overnight from King's Cross, which arrived at the town at 7.05 am *en route* to Dundee. There was a gap in the middle of the day from 10.43 am to 1.40 pm, when a Stirling to Anstruther service called, followed by the 3.08 pm and 4.34 arrivals. The more intensive evening service then followed with the final down train departing from Burntisland at 8.05 pm. The up commuter service mentioned above was followed at 9.37 am by a train to Dunfermline Lower and at 10.50 am and 11.55 am with Edinburgh trains. A Dundee Tay Bridge to Glasgow Queen Street train called at 1.35 pm followed by an Anstruther to Edinburgh train at 2.02 pm. A service from Perth via Ladybank called at 7.50 pm and the final up train of the day called at 9.07 pm bound for Dunfermline Upper.

The *West Fife Echo* related an incident on the Kirkcaldy and District Railway in its edition of 20th February, 1907 which emphasised the severity of the winters and the privations of workmen at the time.

PS *William Muir* with single funnel at Granton.   *Alan Brown Collection*

PS *William Muir* at Granton in the late 1920s.   *Douglas Yuill Collection*

A sad accident resulting in the death of two lads occurred on the mineral railway near Auchtertool at about 6.15 am on Wednesday morning. The lads were Andrew Mackay, 15 years of age, pit drawer, son of David Mackay, carter, Auchtertool, and John Grieve, 17 years of age, pit pony driver, son of David Grieve, weighman, Auchtertool. Along with two other lads named Dempster and Ballingall, Mackay and Grieve were proceeding to their work at the Lochhead pit of the Lochgelly Iron and Coal Company. The four were walking abreast on the railway bowing to the wild blizzard which was raging at the moment, they did not hear the approach of a single engine travelling in the direction of Cowdenbeath, which overtook them. Mackay and Grieve were killed instantly. Dempster was also struck, but only slightly and pushed out of the way. His injuries were trifling and Ballingall escaped unhurt.

The PS William Muir

The Forth ferry continued to operate a passenger service with the faithful PS *William Muir*. Services in 1900 were advertised as follows:

From Granton
(weekdays)   7.00, 9.35 am, 12.15, 2.25, 4.00, 5.45, 7.15 pm
(Sundays)   7.50 am, 1.00, 5.05 pm

From Burntisland
(weekdays)   8.00, 11.36 am, 1.35, 3.15, 5.00, 6.30, 8.10 pm
(Sundays)   9.25 am, 2.00, 6.20 pm

Fares were: Single Cabin 10*d*., Steerage 5*d*., Return Cabin 1*s*. 6*d*., Steerage 10*d*.
Passenger boats will sail as above, or sooner or later as the trains arrive. Tickets for the ferries must be taken out at the Railway Offices.

Having been put on the Granton crossing in 1879 and operating the passenger crossing virtually solo since the opening of the Forth Bridge, by the turn of the century the *William Muir* was showing signs of her age. However, the NBR was slow to progress repairs and after much delay, the boat was sent in 1909 to A. & J. Inglis of Glasgow for examination and a full report, involving a three day journey round Scotland in each direction. They declared that the hull was in satisfactory condition. Tenders were sought from a number of local repairers, including Caledon Shipbuilding of Dundee and Hawthorn's. The latter intimated that it did not repair paddle steamers but an estimate of £8,000 was submitted in June 1909 from Ramage and Fergusson for repairs to the boat.

The NBR was anxious to have the *William Muir* out of service for the shortest possible time, and so a temporary replacement was sought for the crossing during her absence. Previously, in 1898, a replacement had been found from the fleet of the Galloway Saloon Steam Packet Company of Leith, by now part of the North British Steam Packet Company. The temporary vessel on that occasion was the PS *Wemyss Castle*, which was somewhat limited in capacity, restricted to passengers only. The congestion at Waverley station and on the lines over the Forth Bridge, resulting from the growth of services from Edinburgh, led many passengers to prefer the ferry crossing and the small *Wemyss Castle* was not popular during her brief tenure.

To cover the absence of *William Muir* during her latest overhaul, Nichol of Dundee offered a boat at £10 per day, but the NBR once more hired from Galloway. The stand-in was PS *Edinburgh Castle* and she was hired for £15 per day. Scott and Co. of Kinghorn (successors to John Key) built *Edinburgh Castle* in 1886 for M.P. Galloway. The *William Muir*, however, remained on station until January 1910.

A mishap with castings delayed matters further and meant that although she was sent to Leith on 15th January, 1910 she was not handled until the following month. When the repairers examined the boat more closely, it was found that much heavier repairs were required. Removal of internal panelling revealed that 21 hull plates were badly damaged and needed to be renewed. Even a revised estimate for the hull (£6,600) and the engines and boilers (£6,275) was insufficient, and costs rose further at the beginning of 1910, eventually reaching £16,000. The subsequent replacement of engines and paddles resulted in an increased space on deck for motor vehicles, which were now being transported across the Granton crossing to Burntisland. The rebuilt *William Muir* was given sea trials on the Forth on Saturday 14th April, 1910 and accepted back into service. Ramage and Fergusson had to pay a penalty of £1,125 for her late return. The regular passengers on the Granton to Burntisland crossing might have had some difficulty in recognising their favourite boat, for it had a substantially different look. One of her two funnels had been removed and the other set back nearer the stern.

In 1917 the boat was pressed into war service as a minesweeper, working out of Sheerness and returned once more to the Forth and her regular duties in May 1919. The *William Muir* remained a popular craft right up to the end of her working life. One of the popular journeys she made was on a Sunday evening, when Scottish licensing laws prohibited the sale of alcohol except to bona fide travellers. This law encouraged the citizens of Edinburgh to travel across the Forth on the ferry and take advantage of the hotels in Burntisland. Drinkers had to sign in, with their address, and so the journey brought about much consumption of beer and spirits (and welcome profits to Burntisland licensees). The last crossing to Granton was made by many who might be more prone to *mal de mer* than at other times!

On retirement on 2nd March, 1937, the *William Muir* had completed an estimated 80,000 crossings and sailed 800,000 miles, her final voyage on the Forth being upstream to Charlestown, where she was broken up. She was replaced by TSS *Snowdrop*, a former Mersey ferry built for the New Brighton to Liverpool crossing operated by Wallasey Corporation. Her arrival on the Forth was less than auspicious for the transfer of *Snowdrop* from the Mersey to the Forth was undertaken by tug round the North of Scotland. There she broke loose from her tug, *Warrior*, in the Pentland Firth and drifted without power or light for two days, before rescue.

Although renamed after a previous Forth ferry, TSS *Thane of Fife*, the new vessel could not live up to her predecessor. But then, no boat could have entered the affection of her passengers as much as the '*Willie Muir*', as she was affectionately known. Ironic that the best known boat was named after one of the least known Directors of the North British Railway. The replacement boat's service was not a lengthy one, the crossing being suspended by the company in March 1940 to permit the naval use of the port of Granton. Closure of the Granton to Burntisland crossing was announced in 1946.

Reinstatement of the service was attempted in 1952 using four wartime tank landing craft as a car ferry. The boats, purchased by a Kirkcaldy businessman, were named MV *Bonnie Prince Charlie*, MV *Eriskay*, MV *Flora Macdonald* and MV *Glenfinnan*. The boats were substantially refitted at Port Glasgow including side access ramps and saloon to carry 40 cars and up to 400 passengers. They used the former passenger ferry ramp at Burntisland for a few months, but mechanical problems led to the abandonment of the service at the end of the year. Optimism over the crossing grew in 1990 when Forth Ferries Limited proposed a new service with a catamaran. The *Spirit of Fife* had a capacity of 250 passengers, many more than potential traffic might suggest, but even with a regular bus connection from Granton to Edinburgh city centre and cruises on the Forth, the venture was unsuccessful.

The 1914 Burntisland Collision

One accident, which will always be associated with Burntisland, took place on Tuesday 14th April, 1914, a few months before the outbreak of World War I. Unfortunately, it is remembered more for the locomotive that was involved than for the severity of the collision, which resulted in a carriage fire and two fatalities. Relating the events surrounding the accident gives a clearer picture of railway operations at the time and the pressures which railway servants were under.

The express train involved was the down 8.00 pm departure from King's Cross, which was due to leave Waverley at 3.55 am for Dundee and Aberdeen. This train carried both sleeping cars and ordinary coaches of East Coast Joint Stock (ECJS) but was run mostly to carry parcels, mail and newspapers in a series of brake vans. It had been hauled by the Great Northern Railway from King's Cross to York, and then handed over to the North Eastern, which, as was normal, provided motive power for the train through to Waverley.

A North British Atlantic, No. 872 *Auld Reekie*, had taken over at the head of the train at Waverley and had eight vehicles behind it as she left 26 minutes late at 4.21 am. The Atlantics were the pride of the line, resplendent in the bronze green livery of NBR passenger locomotives and worked the company's most important trains. The Atlantics were designed by W.P. Reid for the NBR express services through the borders and over the East Coast main line to Aberdeen. The early trials of these engines had resulted in damage to the track at Burntisland and Kinghorn, forcing Reid to issue the instruction that all speed limits must be adhered to. This included the 25 mph restriction through the Burntisland curves.

Auld Reekie had been built as a saturated steam engine by the North British Locomotive Company in July 1906 (works No. 17373), although later fitted with superheater. The weight of the locomotive was 74 tons 8 cwt and the six-wheel tender 45 tons 8 cwt, a combined total of 119 tons 16 cwt. The North British Atlantic was hauling the following coaches:

NBR 4-4-2 No. 872 *Auld Reekie* setting out from Edinburgh Waverley.
James F. McEwan Collection/T25/15/1272

NBR 4-4-2 No. 872 lies on its side at Burntisland Links, following the 1914 accident. NBR 0-6-0
No. 793 is in the background with the breakdown train.   *Ken Falconer Collection*

ECJS	No. 41	8 wheel bogie	3rd class coach	27 tons 5 cwt	gas lit
ECJS	No. 7	8 wheel bogie	brake	27 tons 0 cwt	electrically lit
NBR	No. 6	8 wheel bogie	brake van	24 tons 2 cwt	gas lit
NER	No. 42	6 wheel	brake van	13 tons 12 cwt	gas lit
ECJS	No. 5	8 wheel bogie	brake van	27 tons 0 cwt	electrically lit
ECJS	No. 379	8 wheel bogie	3rd class coach	28 tons 13 cwt	electrically lit
ECJS	No. 169	8 wheel bogie	sleeping car	32 tons 19 cwt	electrically lit
ECJS	No. 142	12 wheel bogie	brake composite	37 tons 0 cwt	electrically lit

The total weight of the train was thus 217 tons 11 cwt, well within the capacity of the locomotive, which for the Aberdeen road was 345 tons. There were 39 passengers on board, 12 in the front coach, six sleeping car passengers and 21 in the coaches at the rear. Even at that early hour, the locomotive and train would have made an impressive sight as they pulled away from Waverley and through the cutting below Edinburgh Castle into the tunnel toward Haymarket.

The first rays of light were just beginning to appear through the slight mist in the sky. Eastern Scotland can be chilly at that time of the morning even in April and this day was no different. As it was, the rails were already showing the first glistening signs of dew. Driver John Dickson of Aberdeen knew that in these conditions it would be virtually impossible to make up time on the twisting road through Fife to Dundee. His mate, William McDonald of Arbroath, would have had enough of a problem firing the Atlantic, which was noted for its rolling and pitching motion, since these engines were greedy for coal. If trying to lessen some of the deficit would be an impossible task, the 59-mile journey would be covered in the booked time of 83 minutes. One particularly difficult stretch of line was that from Aberdour to Burntisland, where a ruling gradient of 1 in 100 had eight reverse curves in the space of 2½ miles and the station speed restriction. At least the mist was beginning to clear as they crossed the bridge, thanks to a stiff breeze coming down the river.

Ahead of this train was the nightly class 'A' goods from Carlisle to Dundee, which had left on schedule at 9.45 pm behind No. 367, travelling through the Scottish borders by the Waverley route to Edinburgh and then onwards over the Forth at the regulation 40 mph. This train often ran late and was booked to leave Edinburgh at 3.42 am ahead of the express, which ran to time more often than not. Although the goods was timetabled to shunt to allow the passenger to pass at Burntisland, the express would often catch up sooner and Dalmeny or Inverkeithing were more likely to be the passing points. However, on the morning of 14th April, the goods train driver, Henry Hodge, commented to his fireman, John Coulthard, that it looked likely to be Burntisland where the operation was undertaken. Departure of the goods from Edinburgh was actually only 21 minutes late, at 4.03 am, still ahead of the express. The train consisted of 41 four-wheel wagons, 6 six-wheel vans and a 14 ton North British brake van, hauled by an unrecorded 0-6-0 tender engine.

Before Inverkeithing, John William Adams, the attendant in the sleeping car, set off to make a regular check of the train, moving forward into the third class coach. His six passengers were all in the sleeping berths, five from King's Cross and one who had joined at York. Adams had been an attendant on this run for 17 years and probably knew every inch of the route as well as the enginemen.

A steam crane begins recovery operations after the 1914 accident, the Roundhouse is in the
background.   *Ken Falconer Collection*

NBR eight-wheel brake van No. 6, propped up and telescoped into ECJS brake van No. 7 (*left*).
                                                                          Ken Falconer Collection

In the ECJS brake van No. 5 was guard George Young, who was in charge of the train, having been one month as a regular on the Aberdeen road. He had carried out his usual duty of testing the vacuum brake before leaving Edinburgh and found that it fell from 18 inches to 13 inches then returned to normal on closing. He immediately occupied himself from Edinburgh sorting the mail, which was in his van. In the NBR brake, was William Trotter, a passenger guard who had worked on the North British for 16 years. He too was a regular on the route, and was the second guard that night, preparing the mailbags, newspapers, parcels and luggage for the next station stop at Dundee.

For both trains, all seemed comparatively normal as each came off the Forth Bridge in turn and began the descent to Fife, the goods at 4.19 am and the express just 21 minutes later, at 4.40 am. By this time, the signalman at Burntisland East had been notified that the goods would need to be shunted to allow the express to pass. At Burntisland, a great deal of railway activity was carried on through the night and the signal cabins remained open for 24 hours. The whole of the East Coast main line was operated by block telegraph.

There were coal trains to handle from the harbour and goods trains in the yard. The shunting of the class 'A' goods for Dundee that morning was just one more routine. This could be performed at Burntisland East junction where there was the option of drawing the goods beyond the crossover and then backing it into the harbour branch, a safe option, or simply crossing onto the up main line. The level of traffic usually determined which action the East signalman would take.

On the morning of 14th April, Charlie Stewart was yard marshalman at Burntisland, controlling the movements between harbour, goods yard and the main line. He had several trains under his control around four o'clock, working closely with Roderick Fraser, the signalman at Burntisland East cabin. Fraser had been a signalman for 13 years, although he had been at Burntisland East for only seven weeks. Such was the level of traffic that East cabin was within sight of Junction cabin and activity in the congested harbour area could be slow due partly to goods movements being restricted to 5 mph over the public level crossing at Forth Place where passengers traversed for the ferry.

In Burntisland goods yard that morning was the regular Dundee to Kipps goods train. It had finished shunting and was being drawn clear and onto the up main line by one of the yard pilots. There were also two mineral trains moving from the harbour to the yard on completion of their unloading onto a ship in the West dock. In order to accommodate the Dundee goods, Fraser and Stewart devised a plan to dispatch the goods to Kipps and allow the Dundee to draw back into the yard. At 4.44 am, Hodge, the latter's driver, was shown a white light from the cabin as he approached the East starter, which showed clear. In response, he pulled forward beyond the points for the harbour branch, and to await a hand signal from Fraser to shunt his train. As part of the agreed plan, the pilot was hauling the Kipps train out onto the up main line at the same time, ready for dispatch. William Gelletly, this train's driver, noted that the Dundee was on the down line as he was hauled onto the up.

Fraser had asked Thomas Watt, the signalman at Burntisland Junction (456 yards to the south-west), to hold the first coal train, which was on its

ECJS eight-wheel third class coach No. 41 lies on its side alongside NBR Atlantic No. 872.
Ken Falconer Collection

ECJS coach No. 41 lies beside the tender of NBR No. 872 on Burntisland Links.
Ken Falconer Collection

way from the West dock sidings to the East dock sidings. The cabin was one of the oldest on the route and existed until 26th April, 1936. In 1914, the Junction cabin had 38 levers, 13 of which were spare, and controlled the entry to this section of the harbour branch and locomotive sidings as well as the main line east from the station. Holding the coal train would thereby leave space for the Dundee goods to shunt onto the harbour branch. Fraser then dispatched the up goods and it entered the Burntisland Junction block section at 4.45 am.

Thus the way might have been clear for the Dundee, had it not been that the coal train from Burntisland West docks had been allowed to proceed and was entering the yard, therefore blocking the space for Hodge's train. Fraser was left with no alternative but to shunt the goods train on the up line, once the Kipps goods was clear of the section. There was a delay of two or three minutes during which time the new plan was communicated to Stewart and Watt, and the Kipps train was cleared back to Burntisland East. These were two critical minutes for by now, 4.47 am, the express was approaching. To driver Hodge's surprise, when he was signalled to shunt, he did not cross into the harbour branch but was taken down to the west end crossover, and onto the up line.

At Burntisland Junction, Watt had accepted the express from Newbiggin, the cabin 1,600 yards to the south-west of Burntisland Junction and under the control of John Aitchison. The time was 4.42 am and Watt offered the train on to Fraser at East cabin at 4.44 am, but Fraser refused to accept the train since the Dundee goods was blocking the down line. The express passed Newbiggin as 4.49 am, and Watt once more offered the train to Fraser, who once more refused it. Watt re-offered the train immediately and was refused a third time. In fact, he was on the telephone to Fraser at the same time over the shunting of the Dundee train. He knew what was taking place at Burntisland East, and in the growing morning light, could have made out the shape of the train on the down line. When the phone conversation was over, he lowered his up home and starter signals to clear the goods.

This was followed by an acknowledgement of 'train entering section' sent by Aitchison at Newbiggin and Watt then lowered his down home signal. To leave it at danger would have brought the express to a standstill. Watt then cleared the down starter although the down distant for Burntisland East home would have remained at danger, locked by the East home signal which itself was locked by the reversed west crossover. In Fraser's cabin, the track circuits rang a bell, which indicated to him that the express was approaching.

Gelletly, on the Kipps goods, now heading south out of the station limits towards Newbiggin, saw the express on the opposite track and remarked to his fireman, William Cairns,'Here's the fast coming. They must have got rid of the Carlisle (the Dundee goods) very quickly'. The speed limit through the long left-hand curve of Burntisland station was 25 mph and John Dickson slowed No. 872 in observance. Dickson was expecting the Dundee goods to be shunted at Burntisland as it had not yet been passed and therefore was especially looking out for the Junction home and the East distant (both signals were on the same post). The former was at clear, and so he would have proceeded at normal speed.

Above: Workmen examine the locomotive after the 1914 accident.
Ken Falconer Collection

Right: NBR brake van No. 6 supported by timbers where it breached the wall of Burntisland Links.
Ken Falconer Collection

Below: The wall at Burntisland Links which was breached by the 1914 accident, the Roundhouse water tower is in the background.
J.F. McEwan/N3704

Fraser was watching the Dundee goods set back and became aware of the impending collision. Glancing to his left, he saw No. 872 pass under the Lammerlaws Road bridge and approach the goods locomotive as it was setting back at about 5 mph through the crossover. Dickson passed the termination board for the speed limit opposite the coaling stage in the locomotive yard and gave a short whistle then began to pick up speed. He saw the red tail light on the brake van of the Dundee goods, which was moving slowly along the up line, but had no idea that the locomotive was still on the down line having just reached the crossover points.

Hodge was alone on the footplate of the 0-6-0, Coulthard having gone to the East cabin in compliance with rule 55. Coulthard had just entered the cabin when he saw the overnight train. 'Here's the express coming', he said, to which Fraser could only utter, 'Oh, my God!' Fraser had left his home signal at danger to protect the goods manoeuvre, but with the Junction's distant 'off', Dickson on board No. 872 had believed that the road was clear. Hodge, meantime attracted by the sound of a short whistle from the direction of the station, looked out of his cab and noticed the Atlantic by now about 200 yards away. The morning breeze was drifting the steam from the smokebox over the cab. Hodge opened his regulator to increase the speed, but this had not taken effect when the NBR Atlantic struck the goods locomotive at 4.51 am. According to a report in the *Railway & Travel Monthly*, 'a railway official gave it as his opinion that the difference of a foot would have meant safety for the express'.

Driver Bob Scott had booked off around 4.30 am from Burntisland locomotive depot after more than 11 hours on duty. He was walking home, across the Lammerlaws Bridge, when he heard the whistle blast from the express and idly stopped to look over the parapet on the north side. What he saw gave an unforgettable sight.

The 4-4-2 glanced off the goods engine, rode upwards and fell to the left over a low retaining wall topped by railings and landed full broadside two feet below the railway on the golf links. The soft ground offered little resistance and the locomotive ploughed into the surface of the links, throwing both soil and stone from the wall over some distance. Driver Dickson and fireman McDonald were thrown from the footplate, and were crushed to death beneath the locomotive. The tender was dragged behind at a right angle to the locomotive and instantly steam covered the scene. The first coach, (No. 41) was badly damaged, falling to the left and at an angle to the tender. Its sides were smashed in, as were several of the internal partitions. Four of the 12 occupants were seriously injured, the others suffering only minor cuts and bruises. The impact fractured two of the pipes from the three gas cylinders beneath the coach. Flames, one foot long, issued from them and set fire to the splintered woodwork of the coach.

The second vehicle, van No. 7, left its bogies and was pushed against the tender. The rear of this van and the front of the following, No. 6, were telescoped by about 10 feet, both of them leaning over the low wall. The fourth van remained on its wheels but also had both ends crushed. The fifth van lost its leading wheels, but the three coaches remaining stayed on the track.

Hodge stepped, unhurt, from his locomotive which had remained upright although the impact had pushed one of its sets of driving wheels off the track.

Inside the cab, Hodge had been surrounded by glass and splintered wood along with steam from the blower cock, which had been knocked off in the collision. He was joined by Coulthard who ran from the cabin and immediately began assisting the passengers in the leading coach, some of whom were lying under the wreckage. Bob Scott who had run down from the bridge helped him and both of them took water from the overturned tender to extinguish the fire in the partitions at the centre of coach No. 41. Together they assisted a passenger with an injured leg.

William Trotter, the guard in No. 6 had reached the scene by this time having resorted to climbing through the window of the jammed door on his van. His was the only vehicle in the train with a fire extinguisher and he applied it to the flaming gas jets. As the supply of gas kept feeding the flame, he attempted to wrench the pipe away from the bodywork, but suffered a burnt hand for his efforts. The flame went out only when the flow of gas had been exhausted from the cylinders. Fortunately, all the passengers had by then been extricated.

Further help came from the NBR works almost opposite the accident scene and from the townspeople living nearby who had heard the crash. David Cranston, the Dundee goods guard, reached the scene to find between 15 and 20 men rescuing passengers and putting out the fire. He helped Coulthard and Scott to take the injured passenger to the workshops opposite.

Young, the senior guard on the express, looked out of his van to see that he was alongside the goods engine, the frames of which had been damaged. He met Trotter who was running forward with the fire extinguisher. 'This is terrible', he said, 'I'll have to go back and protect the train'. He took three detonators from his van and ran back towards Burntisland Junction signal cabin, where he placed them on the track 10 yards apart. Then he went to the cabin and first called to the signalman, before entering the cabin to find it empty. At the foot of the stairs, Thomas Watt was returning from the accident scene in a very nervous state. He told Young that he had made a mistake by taking both the home and starting signals off. Two other people came up, and Young left Watt in their care while he went back to the crash. Later, on returning to the cabin, Young found Watt alone and in despair.

The passengers in the sleeping car were little disturbed by the crash, two of them had to be wakened to be made aware of the disaster which had befallen their train. Adams, the attendant checked on the two first and 19 third class passengers who were in the rear coaches, to find there were no injuries amongst them. Adams then turned off the gas supply to the pantry to ensure no further fires broke out.

When Stewart, the yard marshalman, saw what had happened, he had the presence of mind to send David Dippie, a goods guard, for the local doctor and ran himself to the traffic superintendent's house to tell him of the disaster. At the same time, shunter Harper dashed to the old station building where stretchers and first aid equipment were kept. The remaining passengers were removed from the scene and taken to the company's works nearby to be cared for.

Later that morning large crowds gathered on the Links to examine the scene and observe the recovery of locomotive and train. The third coach, NBR No. 6, was lying at a precarious angle and was immediately propped up with wooden staves. Steam cranes were brought to the scene and began to remove the debris.

A temporary line was laid on the Links to remove the crippled *Auld Reekie* and a re-railing team under the guidance of Bob Edie, put the Atlantic back on the main line, nursing her back to Cowlairs where she was repaired.

The inquiry into the crash was held by Major J. W. Pringle, who concluded that signalman Watt was responsible and had, perhaps inadvertently, pulled off his down distant signal. The inspector noted that Watt had been on duty for about nine hours when the accident occurred, and was anxious not to delay the express. He had had a busy night with shunting movements, telephone calls, (there were three phones and a speaking tube in Burntisland Junction cabin, as well as the four block instruments) and train register to handle. Shunting operations had increased over the previous 10 years averaging 130 each day during the previous week. Pringle recommended that the turn of duty at the Junction box should not exceed eight hours in future. He also noted that a second distant, which was carried on the down starter at Burntisland Junction, had been removed two weeks prior to the accident, although it was not thought to have any bearing on the event.

The major wanted to remove the East down distant, leaving just the Junction down distant but with its operation being jointly controlled by both signalmen. Similar arrangements would apply on the up line with only the East up distant remaining. To prevent fire, he recommended that gas cylinders on coaches should be fitted with cut off valves. Both locomotives were removed from the scene and repaired, later returning to revenue earning service. Major Pringle described the two deceased railwaymen in glowing terms. John Dickson was called 'one of the most reliable drivers in the Company's service' and his fireman, William McDonald as having an 'absolutely clean record'.

The engine continued to operate on the East Coast and Waverley routes and was converted from saturated steam to superheat in June 1921 having its Westinghouse brake removed in 1931. It was withdrawn as LNER No. 9872 in August 1935.

Atlantics continued on the express service to Aberdeen, making good time on the sinuous route. In 1922, Cecil J. Allen recorded that No. 875 *Midlothian* achieved the 85 minute booking from Waverley to Dundee in 83 minutes. With a load of just 260 tons, the engine reached speeds of 64½ mph between Aberdour and Newbiggin, before slowing for the speed limit through Burntisland.

Burntisland Control

The North British reorganised its train control in 1914, and on 1st October, new districts were brought into existence. The Burntisland District, constituted from that date, comprised the area of Fife south of a line from Springfield, near Cupar, to St Andrews. Also included in the new district were Forth Bridge North signal cabin, the Stirling and Dunfermline lines to Stirling and the EP&DR lines to Perth. The North Fife line from Newburgh to Dundee was excluded, falling into Northern District under William Kettles of Dundee. Burntisland District Control office was established during 1920 in the Forth Hotel adjacent to the pier and the station and placed under the control of John

NBR 0-6-0 No. 1 at Scotland Street on the Granton to Edinburgh line.
Author's Collection

NBR 0-6-0 No. 551 ('J34') shunts the dock roads at Burntisland. Earl of Rosslyn coal wagons are visible in the background.
Bill Lynn Collection

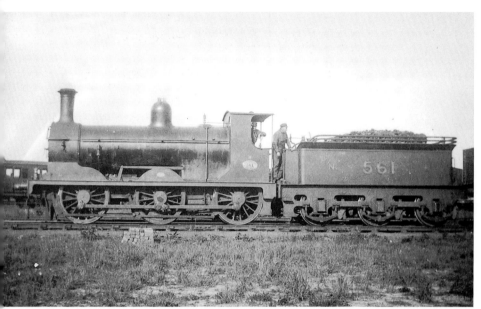

NBR 0-6-0 No. 561 ('J34') at Burntisland.   *Bill Lynn Collection*

NBR class 'D' Drummond 0-6-0 No. 497, at Burntisland coaling stage in 1906. Later LNER class 'J34'.   *A.G. Ellis Collection, courtesy Rex Conway*

Strachan, district traffic superintendent. Formerly, the control had been operated from the original Edinburgh & Northern station building.

The NBR drew up plans in the summer of 1917 to convert two front rooms on the first floor of the Forth Hotel into a full control room, facing onto Forth Place. The new control room was 40 ft 6 in. long and 16 ft wide with the 30 ft control board to the rear wall. The 11 ft ceiling would have made this a well proportioned room to work in and with a billiard room adjacent for recreation, controllers had reasonable working conditions. Additionally, kitchen facilities were provided to the rear. The original plans were not carried out exactly as proposed and the control room itself was built in the eastern half of the first floor, presumably to be directly above the telegraph office. In November 1920, the NBR control system was extended to the Northern district and attached to the district operating superintendent's office at Burntisland. The move brought the new methods of train control, which had been introduced from 1913 in other districts to the north of the Forth.

A fire ravaged the station building at Burntisland in 1914, leaving a large part destroyed. As this occurred early in wartime, rumours were rife and it was believed by some in the town that the damage had been done by enemy arsonists but this was never proved. However, eight German citizens were arrested including the crew of a cargo boat in the East dock. A new station building was considered immediately and plans to reconstruct it in brick were drawn up by William A. Fraser, the NBR engineer-in-chief. James Millar and Sons were offered the contract on 11th December to complete the work for £1,029 4s.

The construction, at the outset of war, of a new naval depot at Rosyth, upstream from Burntisland, brought a number of workmen's trains from Kirkcaldy through the station. Up to 24 each day reached the new port from points around East Scotland, to ensure the rapid completion of the facility.

Motive power at Burntisland was never of the highest order, reflecting the mundane nature of its duties. Prior to the Grouping of the East Coast companies into the London and North Eastern Railway in 1923, an odd assortment of 0-6-0 goods engines worked the lines to the port. Two NBR class 'E' (LNER 'J31'), designed by Thomas Wheatley in 1867, were to be found along with three Holmes class 'D' ('J33'), Drummond class 'D' ('J34'), and seven Holmes class 'C' ('J36').

Burntisland Shipbuilding Company

For years, there was a shipbuilding tradition along the shores of the Forth and as we saw in Chapter One, the 16th century battleship, *Great Michael*, may have been built at Burntisland. Along the shores of the Forth at Kinghorn, John Key and Son had built ships since 1863, including, as we saw in Chapter Five, those for the Forth crossing. John Key spent three years at James Carmichael's engineering works in Dundee, the builders of the first locomotives on the Dundee & Newtyle Railway. He died in 1876 and passed the business to his sons, Andrew and George, as John Key and Sons.

The firm had been taken over by John Scott and Company in 1886 and modernised. A beam crane was built there using girders bought from John Waddell, who had salvaged them from the Tay Bridge after its fall in 1879. The yard had rail access through a trailing branch off the up main line a few yards east of Kinghorn station. After a difficult period, the yard failed in 1900. In a further attempt to revive flagging fortunes, a new business was begun in 1901, this time under the name of John Scott of Kinghorn. However, the yard declined once more and was defunct by 1911, although John Fletcher of Montrose revived it a second time at the end of World War I. This, too, was unsuccessful and only one ship was launched from 1919 until its eventual closure in 1923. The lack of growth at Kinghorn could be ascribed to a new enterprise that was being considered only a few miles upstream.

The land to the west of the docks at Burntisland was much like the original site of the harbour, sheltered from the east but barren ground, rocky and silted up. It was described in *Syren and Shipping* journal dated 14th April, 1920 as having been 'a dreary and uninviting waste showing few potentialities for industrial development', and could not be considered the ideal location to create a shipbuilding operation.

After World War I, the nation had a need to build more ships, to return Britain to the significant trading nation she had been. The outcome was that any suitable and many unsuitable locations were chosen for shipyards. The combination of factors at Burntisland brought about the creation, by brothers Wilfrid and A.L. Ayre, of the Burntisland Shipbuilding Company in 1918. It was an unlikely shipyard, but one that was to remain in existence until the end of the 1960s. Even more remarkable then, that the first ship was launched only 13 months after the work began to construct the shipyard. This method was considered to be opposite to the 'National Plan' which preferred the establishment of the yard before the erection of ships commenced.

The site was cleared in May 1918 and work began to lay out the yard, taking advantage of access from the NBR sidings on the landward side. So keen were the Ayres to start building ships that they brought four railway coaches to the site in August, placing them in an 'H' formation to act as offices until the permanent buildings were complete in September. The keel plate of the first ship, *Sunbank*, 5,400 tons, was laid on 25th June, 1918 with those of sister ships, *Suncliff* and *Sunfield* following shortly afterwards. The three were ordered by Mitchell Cotts and launched on 26th June, 24th October and 24th November, 1919, respectively. Another three ships were launched before the middle of 1920, so fast was the production rate. Using steel plate from Edinburgh steel works, the company was launching a steamer per month at one stage, prompting comment in *Syren and Shipping* that this effort was 'fine work for a new concern'.

The yard was linked to the existing railhead at Burntisland with through connections from the West dock. The company had a travelling crane, which ran on dockside rails and had access to the western quay of the harbour. The Ayres had a busy order book and constructed 322 ships in total, the final launch being the *Helen Miller* for St Vincent Shipping Company. Repairs were also carried out, the first being to SS *Parktown* in 1921. She had entered Burntisland

The land to be taken for the shipyard, May 1918.   *Author's Collection*

Burntisland Shipbuilding Company's yard being laid out in May 1918.   *Author's Collection*

light to load coal but was blown against the West pier by a gust of wind. In order to trim the ship and keep the damage above the waterline, she was loaded with coal and waited only a couple of days for the repairs to begin.

During World War II, several frigates were built at Burntisland, but the need for ships was diminishing. In 1946, the company joined with Hall Russell and Alexander Hall to form the Burntisland Shipbuilding Group, an arrangement that lasted until 1968. The decline of shipbuilding nationally had its effect on the town although up to 800 men were employed there in the 1960s. The loss of £1 million on one contract for the passenger and cargo ship, the *Ohrmazd* built for the West Steamship Company of Karachi, has been blamed for the closure of the yard in 1968.

Coal exports declined from the Fife pits during the 1920s as the mining industry went through a series of damaging blows. The seven-hour day, which had been introduced by the Liberal government, was increased to eight hours. A national miner's strike in 1921, brought about by this move and further action to reduce wages, cut production dramatically as the pits were kept operating by management. Traffic to the ports fell and Burntisland was no different to others in this respect.

Despite a brief period of prosperity, there was a loss of markets in Europe following the rise in reparations from Germany after World War I. As part payment to other European countries, German coal production was increased until, in 1928, it had reached 165 million tons. With the parallel shift to electrical power, markets were lost in Spain and Italy and prices fell. Fife Coal Company reported that Cowdenbeath steam coal for the Danish State Railway was exported at 11s. per ton, below the cost of production and shipment at Burntisland. New markets were found in Brazil and Argentina, taking advantage of the reduction in price. Only one Hamburg industrialist found it cheaper to import from Fife than to tranship German coal by rail and canal to his plant.

During this time, the General Strike of 1926 took place, an event which involved the both railwaymen and miners. The miners stood alone for a total of seven months after others had settled before returning to work, further reducing the traffic through the ports. Britain's return to the gold standard increased overseas prices resulting in more discontent at home. A further blow to the miner was the introduction of mechanisation below ground, although production did increase consequently, improving stocks in the years prior to the outbreak of war for a second time.

The shipment of coal from Burntisland was suspended for strategic reasons during World War II, beginning once more in 1946. The port's days were numbered as tonnages shipped fell below 5,000 tons. The Wemyss railway was able to continue with worthwhile exports and shipment was easier from the Wemyss Private Railway rather than directly off the main line at Burntisland. The turning point in the port's fortunes was in 1956 when coal imports began and, although infrequent, brought about the end of coal handling by 1960.

Prior to then, part of the West dock was leased to the shipbuilding concern and, in June 1952, three hoists were removed to permit this. The remaining three hoists were dismantled during the 1950s and 1960s, leaving bauxite as the harbour's main commodity.

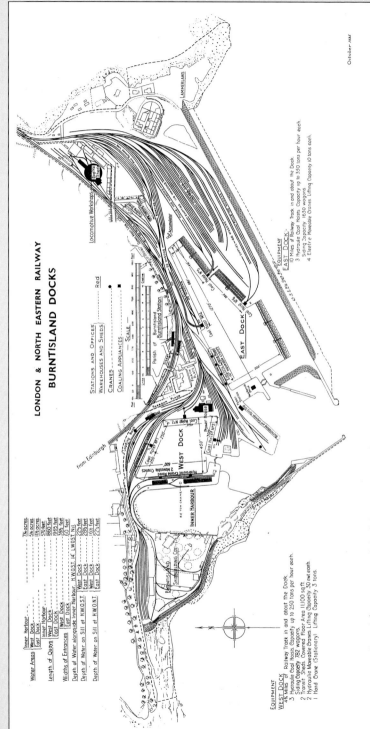

LNER plan of the station and dock lines at Burntisland in 1935.

Post-Grouping Years

After the North British had become part of the wider London and North Eastern Railway (LNER) at the Grouping in 1923, the Burntisland works was reduced to carrying out wagon repairs, having continued to be a source of employment for as many as 300 men in 1921. Locomotive repairs ceased on 15th September, 1923 and all such work went to Cowlairs in Glasgow. At that time, only 53 men were employed at Burntisland on wagon repair, under the charge of one supervisor. Fittingly, in view of the age of the premises, the final locomotive to be repaired there is recorded as Wheatley-designed NBR No. 1122, an 0-6-0 formerly numbered 396 and built in 1867 by Neilson of Glasgow.

As more traffic was dependent on both Methil and Burntisland, Thornton Junction became the main engine shed in Fife. A new shed was built in the early 1930s growing from a four-road building housing 16 engines to a six-road shed for 36. In a reversal of roles, the locomotive shed at Burntisland became a sub-shed of Thornton Junction, in 1933, transferring its complement of nine locomotives to the new structure, giving a total of 86. The Roundhouse was then closed the same year and was demolished soon afterwards. However, the massive stone-built water tower and former entrance to the Roundhouse was retained and served as protection for the locomotives which were stabled at Burntisland.

However, the offices at the old works were retained and served as the base for the Docks Department of the LNER at Burntisland. Under the management of W.S. Grindlay, a small team was responsible for the maintenance of the machinery at the docks, hoists, hydraulics, etc. Amongst the staff were John Nicholson, a wagon repairer who had been injured and became chief clerk and co-incidentally shared the surname of the first locomotive engineer at the works, and father and son Andrew and Charlie Wright.

Familiar NBR types hauled traffic through the town, but in 1934, the LNER tried out a new class. With an unusual wheel formation of 2-8-2, the class 'P2s' were designed by Gresley for the traffic requirements of the demanding road north of Edinburgh, with its twists and turns. The first to be completed was No. 2001, *Cock o' the North*, which was turned out on 22nd May at Doncaster, from where she entered trials on trains to King's Cross. A transfer to Haymarket shed in July allowed trials to be transferred to the Aberdeen road. Six were built in total and later streamlined.

The power of the Mikado showed in the ascent of the incline to the Forth Bridge from a standing start. Its leading truck permitted a reduction in the length of the locomotive, and was intended to lead the eight driving wheels into the tight curves of the road, including that through the sharp curves over the viaduct at Burntisland. Unfortunately, the frames were put under strain and the class was later rebuilt as Pacifics. Another of the 'foreigners' from south of the border was a class of 0-6-0T locomotive that appeared at Burntisland docks, 'J69s', used mainly on shunting duties.

The LNER rationalised the signal cabins at Burntisland in 1936, resulting in the closure of one of the two that controlled the station and docks. Although the

LNER 0-6-0 No. 9159, formerly NBR No. 159 at Burntisland coaling stage.   *Author's Collection*

LNER class 'J33' 0-6-0 No. 9269 (ex-NBR Holmes class 'D') pauses by the 25 mph speed restriction board on the main line at Burntisland to take water on 29th August, 1925.

Bill Lynn Collection

LNER 2-4-0 No. 10249, formerly NBR Wheatley No. 249 at West dock, Burntisland.
Author's Collection

LNER class 'N15' 0-6-2T No. 9079, formerly NBR No. 9, at Burntisland coaling stage.
Author's Collection

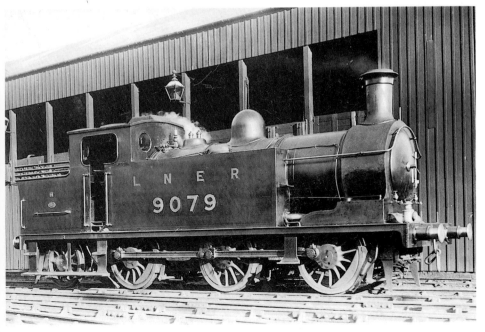

TSS *Thane of Fife,* formerly TSS *Snowdrop* leaves Burntisland for Granton in 1938.
Douglas Yuill Collection

The Bathing Pool, Burntisland in 1937 with the Dock Roads behind.
St Andrews University Library/JV A5275

NBR had referred to signal 'cabin', the LNER used the more familiar term of 'box' to describe them. On Sunday 26th April, 1936, Burntisland Junction box, scene of the 1914 accident, was closed and signalling transferred to Burntisland East box, which was renamed Burntisland Junction. The replacement frame, situated on the up side of the main line to the east of the station and adjacent to the works, had 42 levers (five spare) and in addition, the West dock ground frame had five. The routes under its control were up and down main lines, and sidings at both West dock and wagon repair shop. The Harbour branch, which passed behind the box and lead to the East dock sidings was also under Burntisland Junction with local control from Lammerlaws ground frame nearby. Signals one and five in the latter frame were controlled from Burntisland Junction box.

In 1930, a newspaper article written in the *Fifeshire Advertiser* by William Erskine described the condition of the 1847 station building. Although a little run-down and out of use as a passenger terminal for 50 years, the building was still regularly occupied.

. The station itself was much the same as it still is, the polished stone portico with its weather worn pillars forming the western front. The old ticket or booking office is now utilised as a dwelling place for railway servants and of course, the span of the station roof has gone. The row of old buildings formerly used for miscellaneous purposes still remains, neglected and pointless. Even the good old Bar, which resounded often with the desperate cries of thirsty travellers. A foreign mission station occupies an adjoining room.

The freight service over the Auchtertool branch reduced from the pre-Grouping service of five trains per day in each direction to one in each direction by 1923. The morning weekday train in the up (Cowdenbeath) direction, left Burntisland at 10.35 am and called first at Invertiel Junction to lift refuse traffic for Balbarton siding, near Auchtertool. Balbarton served the Kirkcaldy municipal refuse tip and wagons were shunted for tipping. Once the train reached Foulford Junction at 12.20 pm, it went on to Raith sidings. The afternoon return train left Raith sidings at 1.30 pm reaching Burntisland at 3.50 pm. By 1936, the service was reduced to a trip working to Auchtertool from Burntisland with an extension to Newton or Foulford if required. Raith sidings was where the Fife Coal Company transferred its wagons from Dalbeath and Hill of Beath collieries.

Sunday School and other Excursions

Like many other years, 1936 saw a number of Sunday School excursions. Usually run on a Saturday in late spring, these specials took hundreds of adults and children to a local resort for a picnic and games. Saturday 30th May, 1936 was one such day, and provides us with a fascinating snapshot of a well-planned if sometimes complicated railway operation. The date was the Whitsun holiday in England as well as the British Amateur golf championship at St Andrews, all express trains through Burntisland were strengthened by two coaches to handle the expected golf supporters. A further two relief trains ran in the evening from Dundee via Leuchars Junction to Thornton and then directly to Glasgow to take the crowds home. There was even a military special to fit in from Aberdeen to camp at Knowesgate near Scotsgap in Northumberland, but like the golf reliefs, it was not scheduled to stop at Burntisland.

Activity at Burntisland centred round Sunday School specials, and, although an obvious destination, the town saw both arriving and departing services! Carnock Parish Church Sunday School of Oakley brought 150 adults and 200 children to sample the delights of Burntisland Links and sands. The train ran as empty coaching stock from Alloa at 1.05 pm departing Oakley at 1.30 pm and, running through Dunfermline Upper and Lower, reached the main line via Inverkeithing North and East junctions, arriving at Burntisland at 2.02 pm. The party left at 6.40 pm returning to Oakley at 7.12 pm, the empty train then returning to Dunfermline Upper.

The same day, Erskine United Free Church Sunday School left Burntisland at 1.30 pm with 100 adults and 100 children, for Dunfermline Lower, running the opposite way to the Oakley party. After no doubt an enjoyable afternoon at either Pittencrieff Glen or Comely Park, the group departed at 7.00 pm reaching Burntisland at 7.35 pm During the day, the empty train was stored at Dunfermline Upper station yard.

Burntisland was the starting point for another Sunday School special, carrying parties from Rosslands Church, Kinghorn and Victoria Road Sunday School, Kirkcaldy to Markinch. The empty train left Burntisland yard at 2.00 pm, acquiring 150 passengers from Kinghorn, who had reserved compartments at the front of the train and 250 from Kirkcaldy and Sinclairtown, who were located at the rear. Arriving at 2.35 pm, the train went on to Thornton Junction from where it departed at 6.35 pm to collect its passengers reaching Burntisland yard at 7.45 pm. The general populace was treated to an advertised evening excursion from Dysart to Perth via Burntisland, departing from the town at 5.35 pm and reaching Perth at 6.58 pm for a stop of two and a half hours. The return service reached Burntisland at 10.51 pm.

Monday 1st June was the Fife Miner's Gala day with both traditional outings and a miner's demonstration in Pittencrieff Glen, Dunfermline. In order to ascertain how many people were travelling on that day the district operating superintendent at Burntisland required station masters to submit an estimate of passengers by Saturday 30th May and to ensure that they had sufficient tickets available. Traffic movements would have been most involved that day including the use of the Old station at Cowdenbeath (although not the Invertiel branch) and once again, Burntisland was a favourite destination for some of the special trains, as follows:

Lochgelly to Burntisland

Dunfermline Upper	dep. ecs	9.30 am			
Lochgelly	dep.	10.04	Burntisland	dep.	6.50 pm
Thornton West Jn	pass	10.15	Kirkcaldy	pass	7.02
Thornton South Jn	pass	10.17	Thornton South Jn	pass	7.11
Kirkcaldy	pass	10.29	Thornton West Jn	pass	7.13
Burntisland	arr.	10.39	Lochgelly	arr.	7.25
Dunfermline Upper	arr. ecs	11.15	Dunfermline Upper	arr. ecs	8.00

Cowdenbeath New to Aberdour

Dunfermline Upper	dep. ecs	10.30 am			
Cowdenbeath New	dep.	10.59	Inverkeithing	dep. ecs	5.40 pm
Lochgelly	dep.	11.06	Aberdour	dep.	5.55
Cardenden	dep.	11.11	Burntisland	dep.	6.01
Thornton West Jn	pass	11.20	Kinghorn	dep.	6.08
Thornton South Jn	pass	11.22	Kirkcaldy	dep.	6.15
Dysart	dep.	11 29	Sinclairtown	dep.	6.20
Sinclairtown	dep.	11.33	Dysart	dep.	6.24
Kirkcaldy	dep.	11.38	Thornton South Jn	pass	6.30
Kinghorn	dep.	11.45	Thornton West Jn	pass	6.32
Burntisland	dep.	11.51	Cardenden	dep.	6.42
Aberdour	arr.	11.57	Lochgelly	dep.	6.48
Inverkeithing	arr. ecs	12.10 pm	Cowdenbeath New	arr.	6.54
			Dunfermline Upper	arr. ecs	7.10

Cardenden to Kirkcaldy

Dunfermline Upper	dep. ecs	11.05 am			
Cardenden	dep.	12.20 pm	Kirkcaldy	dep.	6.10 pm
Lochgelly	pass	12.27	Kinghorn	dep.	6.17
Lumphinnans Ctl Jn	pass	12.29	Burntisland	arr.	6.22
Cowdenbeath Old	dep.	12.35		dep.	6.23
Cowdenbeath S. Jn	pass	12.38	Aberdour	dep.	6.30
Crossgates	dep.	12.41	Inverkeithing E. Jn	pass	6.37
Townhill Jn	pass	12.44	Inverkeithing N. Jn	pass	6.39
Dunfermline Lower	arr.	12.47	Dunfermline Lower	arr.	6.45
	dep.	12.49		dep.	6.46
Inverkeithing N. Jn	pass	12.53	Townhill Jn	pass	6.51
Inverkeithing E. Jn	pass	12.54	Crossgates	dep.	6.56
Aberdour	dep.	1.03	Cowdenbeath New	dep.	7.01
Burntisland	arr.	1.08	Lochgelly	dep.	7.07
	dep.	1.09	Cardenden	arr.	7.11
Kinghorn	dep.	1.16	Leuchars Jn	arr. ecs	8.30
Kirkcaldy	arr.	1.21			

(note ecs = empty coaching stock)

The following Saturday, 6th June, Edinburgh Borderer's Union golf club reserved accommodation for 20 adults on the 1.16 pm from Waverley to Burntisland for an outing to the town, returning from Burntisland at 5.58 pm. However a huge train of 730 people set off on a Sunday School special from Penicuik to Dunfermline, Aberdour and Burntisland. Empty coaching stock left Portobello yard at 11.00 am departing Penicuik at 12.35 pm with 250 adults and children from St James the Less for Dunfermline Lower, 250 from North Church for Aberdour and 230 from South

Church for Burntisland. The route was via Niddrie West and the Edinburgh suburban line to Haymarket West Junction. At Dalmeny the Dunfermline portion was detached from the rear of the train, the front portion setting off first to reach Aberdour at 1.55 pm and Burntisland five minutes later. Returning at 7.30 pm, the train oddly was not reunited with the portion from Dunfermline until Niddrie West for the short distance to Penicuik, where arrival was made at 8.48 pm.

A company of 140 adults and 150 children from Greenside Church Sunday School of Alloa spent the afternoon at Burntisland, sharing their train with two other parties who travelled from Dunfermline to Sinclairtown and Aberdour. The train departed empty stock from Kinross Junction to Alloa, leaving the latter at 12.40 pm and reaching Burntisland at 1.50 pm for a six-hour stay. The return trip ended at Alloa at 8.35 pm from where the empty train returned to Kinross Junction. From further afield came another excursion of Sunday School pupils.

Airdrie provided two parties for Burntisland, 300 from Jackson Church left Airdrie South at 10.46 am and were joined by 250 from Caldercruix West Church at Caldercruix. Two further groups travelled to Kinghorn making a total complement of almost 900 people. The journey was involved travelling via Bathgate East Junction to a reversal at Queensferry Junction from where the speed on the freight-only line to Dalmeny Junction was limited to 20 mph. The station master at Kirkliston had to make special arrangements to operate the crossing gates there. The arrival at Burntisland was 12.07 pm leaving eight and a half hours in the town. Another excursion took the same route, departing from Bellshill with 300 members of the Congregational Church, joined at Whifflet by 500 from Garnturk Church, reaching Airdrie by another reversal at Sunnyside Junction and running about 30 minutes behind the preceding train.

St Andrew's Church in Burntisland had its own outing on 6th June. Then 50 adults and 150 youngsters left the town at 1.30 pm, travelling via Dunfermline to Cowdenbeath New, where the party spent 5½ hours at the public park in Perth Road before returning at 7.40 pm for the journey back to Burntisland.

A further special was arranged for a trades' outing of 75 adults and 130 juveniles from Dunfermline to Burntisland departing from the Upper station at 10.50 am and arriving at 11.15 am. The party then walked to Kinghorn from where they returned at 7.22 pm, calling at Burntisland eight minutes later for a 26 minute journey to Dunfermline Upper. Interestingly the empty stock was stabled at Dunfermline Lower during the day and was positioned at Kirkcaldy for the return trip. The evening excursion was from Glasgow Queen Street to Leven, departing at 5.20 pm and reaching Burntisland at 6.48 pm. A particularly late departure from Burntisland at 10.35pm ensured that Glaswegians reached home just after midnight.

On the Sunday School specials, guards were instructed by the LNER management to ensure that doors on both sides of the coaches were locked from the outside before the train started at the respective stations. As reserved coaches were allocated to different parties, beginning at the front of the train, station masters were instructed to ensure that children were positioned at the appropriate part of the platform to assist boarding.

On Saturday 18th July, the Glasgow trades' holidays, know as 'The Fair', brought 12 relief trains north through Burntisland from Glasgow, all but one of them stopping at the town for holidaymakers to alight.

British Railways

Nationalisation having arrived in 1948, the Burntisland depot remained a sub-shed of Thornton (62A in BR days). It lost its steam allocation in 1959, acting as a base for English Electric and Hunslet 0-6-0 diesel shunters until 1966, when the shed closed completely, having been reduced in the years previously to a signing-on point. There had been one main line locomotive allocated in 1948 for use on the aluminium oxide trains from the BAC works nearby.

Wagon repairs continued at Burntisland during British Railways days, being carried out in later years alongside the original Edinburgh & Northern Railway platform. The old station lines also played host to the ex-LNER 'Silver Jubilee' stock in the 1950s and 1960s, when it was withdrawn from the 'Fife Coast Express'.

The station buildings were given a facelift in 1962 and again in January 1986, when a circular plaque was fixed to the down platform wall, commemorating Bouch's Floating Railway. The 'Control' at Forth Hotel was reduced in status in 1965, when the District office, superintendents and clerical staff were moved to Edinburgh. Five years later, at 10.00 pm precisely on 1st February, 1970, all the work of Burntisland Control was absorbed into the Edinburgh communications centre. Forth Hotel was placed on a care and maintenance basis, looked after by station staff, until by 1997 it had deteriorated so much that demolition was necessary. A new building in the style of Downie's stables next door has since been erected providing additional flats for the town.

The working of the harbour branch was laid out in the appendix to the British Railways' working timetables. Train movements remained much as before with westbound trains confined to the 'ingoing' line and eastbound trains to the 'outgoing' line. This applied to traffic between Lammerlaws ground frame and the West dock sidings. Wrong line working was also permitted but only under the permission of the shunter.

Working beyond Forth Place required the drivers and firemen to keep a constant lookout, especially when working over the six crossings on the branch. These were at the following locations:

Goods shed
Steelyard siding (west end)
West shore (north-west corner of West dock)
Top of Ferry pier (near the waiting room)
Shipyard entrance gate
Forth Place

Only the last named had a crossing keeper since it was over a public highway. The keeper was on duty from 8.00 am until 5.00 pm with a one-hour break from noon. On Saturdays, there was no afternoon duty and none on Sundays A second shunter was required to protect unmanned crossings when a train passed over, and ensure that the wagons did not foul the crossing. The limit of wagons in any one lift was 20. At Lammerlaws crossing to the east of the docks, a crossing keeper controlled the passing of trains.

The travelling crane at Burntisland Shipbuilding Company was permitted to work over the lines between the shipyard and the two sidings immediately to the

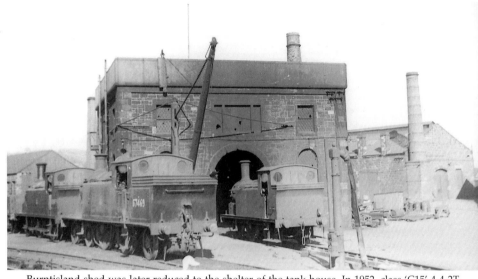

Burntisland shed was later reduced to the shelter of the tank house. In 1952, class 'C15' 4-4-2T
No. 67469 sits with couple of 0-6-0Ts.   *Bill Lynn Collection*

'B1' class 4-6-0 No. 61403 enters Burntisland station with an up train on 25th July, 1959.
Ken Falconer

Class '3F' former Caledonian 0-6-0 No. 57559 pulls a freight away from Granton towards the gasworks.   *Author's Collection*

Two stopping trains pass at Burntisland on 25th July, 1959. 'B1' class 4-6-0 No. 61147 heads towards Kirkcaldy while 'J39' class 0-6-0 No. 64795 returns to Edinburgh with a mixture of coaching stock, probably from the east Fife line.   *Ken Falconer*

Former NBR 0-6-0, class 'J37' No. 64632 draws a train of 'Presflos' from the BAC works across the viaduct at Burntisland on 3rd April, 1965. Freight lines are in the foreground alongside West dock.   *Late J.L. Stevenson, courtesy Hamish Stevenson*

Class 'J38' 0-6-0 No. 65901 is seen with a trip freight at Burntisland. The canopy of the down platform has been removed since this mid-1960s photograph was taken.   *A.A. Maclean*

north of the entrance to the yard and between the shipyard and the quayside lines to the west of the storage sheds on the west quay. Movements had to be accompanied by the company's shunter who had to guarantee that the route was clear and carry a red flag. The Boat Roads, as the entrance to the West dock was known, were singled in the early 1960s, around the same time as the coaling stage and associated sidings were removed. The coaling stage had stood just to the west of Lammerlaws Bridge, between the locomotive sidings and the wagon sidings.

Further alterations occurred in 1969, when the west crossover (No. 18) and points (No. 5) were removed. The pre-1890 Burntisland Junction cabin opposite the coaling stage was demolished shortly afterwards, although one of the early cabins remained in position for many years, boarded up and looking run down. The renamed Burntisland Junction box remained in existence until the resignalling of the Fife Circle line was completed and control was transferred to Edinburgh on 12th December, 1979. The box was demolished soon afterwards. At that time, the Lammerlaws connection was removed and the connection removed in 1969 was re-instated.

The Auchtertool line did not have a prosperous life in later years, particularly as coal mining declined and was severed to the west of Auchtertool in the early 1950s leaving two branches, accessible from either end. An additional factor was mining subsidence, which would add to the cost of maintaining the track for trains that could easily have taken the Thornton route. Traffic in the final years centred on barley for the distillery at Auchtertool but this too diminished at the end of the 1950s. Redundant wagons were stored on the truncated line. The goods depot at Auchtertool was closed by British Railways on 3rd October, 1960. The junction signal boxes closed in 1963, on 5th June (Foulford Junction) and 17th November (Invertiel). The box at Auchtertool had closed many years previously on 28th August, 1923 and was replaced by a ground frame.

A short-lived proposal was suggested in the 1970s, when Mossmoran petrochemical plant was under construction near the remains of the Auchtertool line. A short diversion from a relaid line would connect the plant to the national rail network, but such was the negativity towards rail freight at the time that the proposal was not developed further.

As part of the Fife Council's supportive position on rail transport, new service was created by installing a chord from a new station at Thornton on the former Dunfermline branch to the main line. The result was to enable trains from Edinburgh Waverley to provide a Fife circle service in either direction, travelling to Inverkeithing then either via Dunfermline or Burntisland. In May 1989, new trains, class '150' dmus, replaced the older first generation dmus on the Fife services. These were joined by some class '156' units and the return of older trains to strengthen peak services.

A further accident occurred at Burntisland at the end of the 20th century when a train of loaded merry-go-round coal hoppers (mgr) was derailed on the down side just to the north end of Burntisland station platform, very near to where the 1914 collision had taken place. Coal trains for the Longannet power station, which reached Fife across the Forth Bridge, would have found themselves having to reverse at Dunfermline in order to reach the coastal route to their destination. To avoid the manoeuvre, trains went 'the long way round' the Fife circle through Burntisland, Thornton and Cowdenbeath, in order to have a clear approach to the branch.

Kinghorn station looking towards Kirkcaldy in 1965, with goods facilities still intact.
Bill Lynn Collection

Burntisland through station in 1961, showing buildings on the down side.
James F. McEwan/N3318

A pair of Birmingham RCW type '2' Bo-Bos pass through Burntisland on an Aberdeen-Edinburgh train in the early 1960s. *A.A. Maclean*

Hunslet-built diesel-mechanical 0-6-0 shunter No. D2581 works the sidings behind the works in the early 1960s. The grounded brake van at the rear is of NBR vintage. *A.A. Maclean*

English Electric type '4' (later class '40') 1-Co-Co-1 No. 264 with a northbound class '6' freight c.1970 as it passes the former Burntisland Junction signal cabin, built for the opening of the line and superseded when the extension to the Forth Bridge opened in 1890.　　*A.A. Maclean*

An interior view of the works at Burntisland.   *A.A. Maclean*

Burntisland station from the east in 1977, showing the (now demolished) shelter on the down side.   *Author's Collection*

Burntisland station looking west in 1996.   *Author*

Burntisland station building in BR days. *Iain Sommerville*

'A4' Pacific No. 60009 *Osprey* enters Burntisland on 8th September, 1990 with 'The Forth Centennial' special. *Bill Roberton*

ScotRail class '170' crosses the Links at Burntisland with an Edinburgh to Aberdeen service in October 2000.   *Author*

ScotRail class '150', No. 150 259 departs for Aberdour on a Fife Circle service to Edinburgh, October 2000. The plaque to commemorate the original train ferry to Granton can be seen in the background.   *Author*

At 7 o'clock on the morning of Wednesday 8th July, 1998, as a train of mgr wagons took this route, one of the HAA hopper wagons derailed when passing at the east end of Burntisland station, and ploughed into the trackbed turning over the nearside rail as it did so. The train continued upright until it reached the crossover whereupon the train divided and the rear 16 HAAs with their load of coal cascaded into the Links. Unfortunately, the site was being prepared as an arena for the forthcoming Highland Games, and the occupants of a showman's caravan were surprised at this early delivery of fuel. Swift work by the local authority and Railtrack cleared the debris, although the track was closed for four days. The first train through the repaired section was a GNER London train on Sunday morning. Railtrack have taken the opportunity to remove the crossover and the route was plain-lined. Reports of a company keen to use the docks to bring in powdered chalk by rail for processing and distribution to paper mills raised hopes of the crossover being reinstated.

At Kinghorn, the proximity of a school to the branch line tunnel under the main street prompted fears of gas build up and 950 cubic metres of concrete were pumped into it in July 1986. This sealed up the tunnel and blocked off the Binn Oil Company branch for all time.

The harbour at Burntisland saw the demolition in 1978 of the rail embankments which led to the coal hoists at the East dock and the replacement of the dock gates to the East dock in 1980. The docks went on to become part of Forth Ports, a company which owns harbours at Dundee and Tilbury as well as those around the Forth at Leith, Rosyth, Kirkcaldy and Methil. In 1999, Forth Ports, which opened an office in the 1847 station building, handled a record 55.8 million tonnes of cargo, of which Burntisland handled 244,000 tonnes, an increase of 5 per cent on the previous year.

At the turn of the 21st century, Burntisland benefited from the best rail service the town had seen. ScotRail trains provided a frequent service to Edinburgh, Dundee and other towns in West Fife on the Fife circle. A new service from Kirkcaldy to Glasgow Queen Street was being developed. Citizens heard the outcome of discussions to re-site the station nearer the Links and the leisure centre, with better access from the town, improved security and parking for the commuter service to Edinburgh.

The plaque to commemorate the original train ferry to Granton, erected on the refurbishment of Burntisland station in January, 1986.   *Author*

ScotRail class '150', No. 150 259 enters Burntisland on a Fife Circle service to Edinburgh, October 2000.   *Author*

ScotRail class '150', No. 150 254 enters Kinghorn station with a Fife Circle service to Kirkcaldy, October 2000.   *Author*

Chapter Seven

Industrial Railways of the District

Newbiggin Limestone Mine and Quarry

Situated about one mile to the west of Burntisland and north of the A921 to Aberdour lay the Newbiggin mine. It exploited the Burdiehouse limestone layer to be found throughout Fife, this being a thick seam, of calcium carbonate, over 90 per cent pure and very suitable for iron and steel making. Limestone was shipped from Burntisland from around 1742. The Carron Iron Company near Falkirk (founded in 1760) obtained its limestone from the Newbiggin, eventually purchasing the mine in 1808. Then, in 1814, the company bought the neighbouring Newbiggin farm, in order to stable and maintain the horses which worked in the mine. Limekilns were set up near the shore in 1828 to supply lime for agricultural purposes to the farmers of the district.

In 1817, a ¾ mile-long waggonway was established to transfer the limestone to Carron harbour on the Forth and another a few yards upstream. The Carron Iron Company had owned the Tranent waggonway from 1779, a line which transported coal to the shores of the Forth in East Lothian. In 1766, the company had built the Carron waggonway from Kinnaird and Carronhall collieries to its works near Falkirk. The company in fact owned several such waggonways and around 1795 converted some of them to run with iron edge rails rather than wood and iron strip. It would seem reasonable to assume that Newbiggin waggonway was initially installed with iron edge rails. The Carron Iron Company had certainly relaid the Tranent waggon way with cast-iron edge rails as early as 1815.

Later, building stone was quarried from the adjacent quarry and transferred to the harbour and subsequently the railhead.

The earliest mine entrance was a few hundred yards north of the main road and the tram road at first ran south then east before turning south again. At Nine Lums, the waggonway crossed the main road where a rope-worked incline lowered the wagons two at a time to the harbour whilst two empty wagons were returned by gravity from the shore. A brake house was built to keep the speed of descent to walking pace. Properly constructed rails in chairs to enable free running of these wagons would almost certainly have replaced the iron edge rails of the waggonway. This operation lasted from 1856 until 1893. The first line was abandoned in 1896 and a more accessible mine entrance was employed lower down adjacent to the road with two gravity inclines to speed transport to the North British Railway which had arrived in 1890. By 1913, a new tramway was opened to the inclines, passing along the main road for a short stretch.

The North British provided two sidings at Newbiggin, trailing off the down line. One was for the Carron limestone mine and quarry, the other for William Chalmers who operated the stone quarry and traded building stone. Loading chutes were installed over the rails to fill the wagons with the limestone for Carron iron works. Spoil from the inner workings was also transported by rails, being brought from the mine at Nine Lums and deposited on the southern side of the Aberdour road.

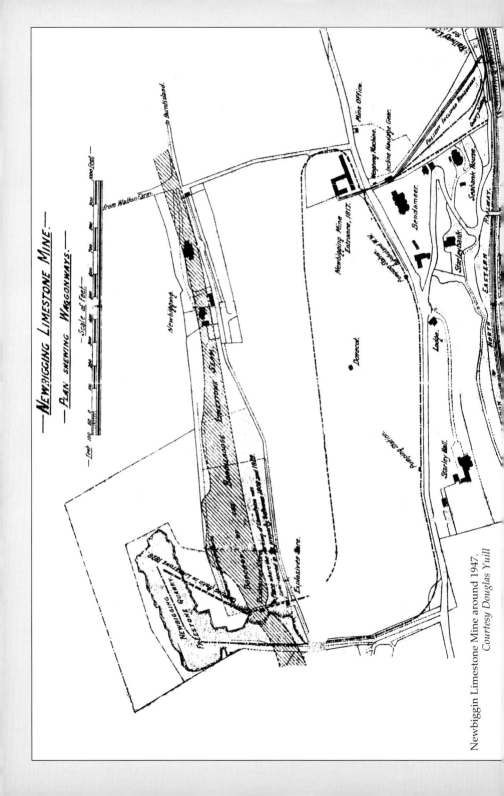

Newbiggin Limestone Mine around 1947.
Courtesy Douglas Yuill

The Fife district register of sidings for the NBR lists two users of the Newbiggin siding, both the Carron Company and William Chalmers, quarrymen. The signal cabin was opened at Newbiggin on 14th August, 1901, replaced with a new cabin located furhter east at the aluminium works in May 1915 and finally closed when Edinburgh took over in 1979. By 1943, the later tramway had been abandoned and additional sidings created by the LNER. The sidings were isolated in the early 1950s when the limestone mine closed.

The Grange Quarry

Limestone was quarried at the Grange, a quarry that had been in existence since before the opening of the Edinburgh & Northern line. It employed up to 100 men at the beginning of the 20th century and was rail linked to the main line. A sale document of the Grange Estate, Burntisland, dated Wednesday 18th December, 1901 described the property as freehold covering an area of 461 acres, located ¾ mile from the thriving town of Burntisland.

The property put up for sale comprised two farms and the stone quarry. The farms were Craigkelly (where the television mast now stands) and Grange farm. Grange Quarry itself claimed to possess 'a considerable depth and area of valuable building and other stone,' which was believed to be 'worked at a very considerable profit'. The lease was effective from 1883 and the tenants, Baird and Stevenson, quarrymasters of Glasgow, had rights to quarry until 1919 during which time the land could be extended. Mr T. Jones produced a report on the condition of the quarry, of which the following is an extract.

> This quarry is situated on the north side of the Great North road, about ¾ mile to the north of the Town of Burntisland.
>
> It is a well-known free stone quarry; the produce (which is mixed with Carboniferous Limestone) having a very wide reputation; it being of excellent character, dressing freely in any direction.
>
> The Quarry has been opened out upon an extensive scale, is about 200 feet deep, and has a present working face of something like 1,000 feet in length.
>
> It is connected with the North British Main Line of Railway by means of Gravitation Inclines, which carry the produce down to a loading Wharf by the side of the Railway.
>
> The tenants have to pay a rental of £2 10s. per acre for the Inclines and Railway South of the Great North Road and £60 per acre for the ground occupied by the Railway or severed in the course of its construction.

A plan accompanying the sale documents illustrated the location of the railway tracks within the quarry but (strangely) failed to show where the sidings on the NBR line were. The internal railway ran in a south-westerly direction from the north and the west of the quarry, crossing the road to Perth before turning south-east and beginning the gravity incline. The incline passed through the land of Kilmundy Quarry, which neighboured Grange. The incline fell below the Aberdour road, where it terminated in siding in the property of Colinswell. This is the logical place for the sidings, next to the main line. In turn, the location would be utilised by the BAC for the aluminium works.

Grange and Kilmundy Quarries at the end of the 19th century.

Courtesy Iain Sommerville

The Binnend Oilworks

To the north of the town of Burntisland, beyond The Binn and only one mile from the centre of the town, lies the valley of the Kinghorn Burn, running east to west. Within this detached valley lay Binnend the village which was home to the Burntisland's short lived oil industry, created to exploit the oil bearing shale which was to be found there. James 'Paraffin' Young virtually single-handedly created the shale oil industry in the 1850s, establishing a patent for the method of low temperature distillation. Once the patent ran out others took advantage of the technique and George Simpson, a speculator from Edinburgh, established The Binnend Oil Company in 1878.

The business did not flourish and was wound up in 1880. The company was sold to John Waddell, an engineer with interests in the construction of many Scottish railways. Amongst his contracts were Tay Bridge station, Dundee and the railways at Leuchars and Tayport. As we have seen, he also built the line from Inverkeithing to Burntisland. Waddell shared the same address as Young's Paraffin Light and Mineral Oil Company. He in turn sold the enterprise to another company formed in August 1881.

The company became the Burntisland Oil Company and improvements were put in hand at once. At the same time, a survey was undertaken for a railway to the works from Pettycur, following a gentler gradient than that which could be taken from Burntisland. Although the site of the works was situated above Burntisland, transport to and from the town was at first by road. A steam-driven traction engine and six road wagons were employed initially to haul materials such as bricks from the North British Railway at the port. This traffic brought concern amongst the members of Burntisland town council that the heavy vehicles would damage the roadway, a situation only slightly assuaged by a charge of one penny per ton on each journey. However, nothing more seems to have happened for another five years, when the company secured land to build a railway to join the NBR at Kinghorn.

The cost of creating the line was estimated at £11,000 initially, although this was subsequently increased to £15,000. This contrasted with the calculated cost of transport by cart, an annual figure of £6,500. Any alternative railway route would have to have been westwards towards the forthcoming Inverkeithing line, and would have produced a gradient of around 1 in 35. The survey was undertaken in June 1886 and work began in September of that year. The autumn commencement was due to a court action by landowner Mr Banks of Grangehill who sought a delay until his crops were harvested.

The contract for construction was believed to have been awarded to John Waddell (who had remained one of the Directors of the oil works), around 100 men being employed throughout the length of the line, which was 2 miles 800 yards from Kinghorn station to No. 2 mine. Waddell took shares in the enterprise as part payment for the work and became an important shareholder. From Kinghorn, at 75 feet above sea level, the line climbed to its highest point at around 250 feet, the gradient averaging around 1 in 50. Perhaps the most significant engineering aspect of the line was the short tunnel under Kinghorn High Street, just after the junction with the North British line. Extensive use of cuttings and embankments was employed and there were seven bridges along the route.

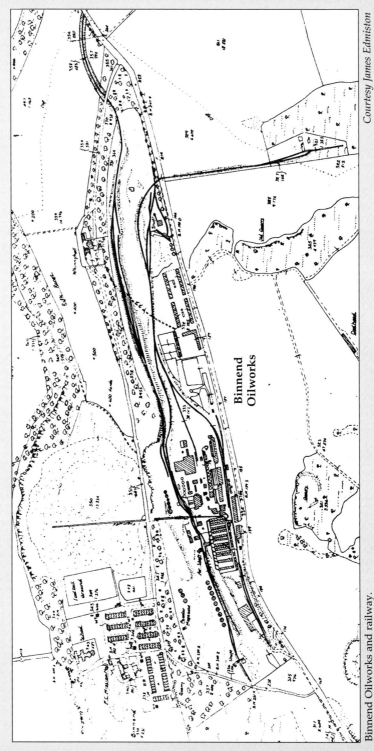

Binnend Oilworks

Binnend Oilworks and railway.

The first recorded train ran in April 1887 with coal for the works and by 2nd May all of the traffic to and from the plant was transported over the new line. Additional sidings were laid within the works proper to move shale to the crushing plant and transport the finished product from the refinery. Later, a single-track spur was laid in May 1892 to transfer shale from No. 4 mine at Grangehill.

The single track line was 2 miles and 800 yards in length from Kinghorn station to No. 2 shale mine. Movement within the mine, to and from the crushing plant and the refinery itself, necessitated additional sidings and loops. The gradient from Kinghorn station to the highest point by the Kirkcaldy road, west of Kinghorn Loch, was approximately 1 in 50. The branch left the main line north of Kinghorn station with a trailing connection off the down line. Passing through a short tunnel, the line then ended in a spur where reversal was required to begin the steep ascent to Binnend. Earthworks were frequent, either as embankments or cuttings before the works were reached. Within the mine and works, the rails were laid on terraces along the hillside. A further length of track was opened at the end of May 1892 to transfer shale from No. 4 pit at Grangehill. Some of the internal workings were by cable haulage.

However the days of shale oil refining were numbered and the company assets were valued in September 1892 at £261,000, of which £22,950 was the worth of the branch railway outwith the works. The whole lot was put up for sale in January 1893, resulting in a new Burntisland Oil Company being created in March, in which John Waddell once more took shares. The whole works were sold at auction in 1894 for £15,000, but the company limped on until 1905.

The village that had grown up around the shale mine and refinery was left to decline until 1954, when the last inhabitant moved out. The rails of the branch line were believed to have remained in place at least until the 1920s.

British Aluminium Company

Opened in 1917, the British Aluminium Company (BAC) works was sited at Kirkton, Burntisland for all the reasons already explained, a sheltered harbour, nearby coalfield with good water supplies and favourable rail connection. The short internal railway came off the siding at Colinswell between Burntisland and Aberdour. The raw material, bauxite, was discovered in and imported from Les Baux in southern France and then later from the Gold Coast (present day Ghana). The bauxite is refined at Burntisland before onward transportation. It is heated in a furnace, slaked with caustic soda to produce aluminium oxide. Both the caustic soda and coal for the furnace were brought by rail. After processing, aluminium oxide was sent onwards by rail to the smelters in Kinlochleven and Lochaber before going on to the rolling mills. The latter went via Glasgow and the West Highland Railway whereas the Kinlochleven traffic was taken via Stirling and the Callander and Oban route to Ballachulish. The original output of 15,000 tons annually was doubled in 1929, rising to 50,000 in the 1930s. The town retained a strategic importance during World War II, as it was the only port to receive cargoes of bauxite during the hostilities. The total output, however, fell to 30,000 tons in 1970.

BAC 0-4-0ST Peckett No. 2, at Colinswell on 4th December, 1967.   *Ken Falconer*

BAC 0-4-0ST Andrew Barclay No. 3 on 4th December, 1967.   *Ken Falconer*

Almost as an act of faith, the company invested £10 million in the plant in the same year to improve output. A particular grade of alumina is produced at Burntisland for use in non-metallic products and this may have helped the plant to survive difficult times. At present 250,000 tons are imported annually, requiring between seven and eight bulk carriers to be handled at the harbour each year. These ships are handled in the river and the ore is transferred to handling barges, which bring it ashore. From there lorries take the bauxite to the plant.

An unfortunate by-product of the process has been a red sludge, which was originally deposited on the seaward side of the plant, then at Whinnyhall on part of the shale works site. This has subsequently been landscaped, the water run-off being recycled.

The LNER built a number of hopper wagons to carry bulk alumina to Kinlochleven. Early wagons were converted from 20 ton eight-plank coal hoppers, with a roof constructed over them. Later 19 wagons were built in 1938 from steel. They carried 15 tons and were of 10 tons tare. Later still, in BR days Covhops replaced these. The non-vacuum-braked stock was spread over a number of Lochaber overnight 'ghost' trains. Initially in LNER days, these were assembled at Sighthill, but in BR days, Cadder yard made up the train. It has been reported that Yoker was used during 1960.

There was a dedicated wharf for bulk carriers in the East dock (nearest the old ferry slipway) and cranes would grab the bauxite from the ships and transfer it to 16 ton standard mineral wagons. In British Railways' days, rakes of 20 to 25 wagons formed a shuttle between the dock and the sidings at the BAC works, returning empty. The empty wagons were cable-hauled by capstan under the cranes to be loaded, and cable-hauled out again before being taken by main line train to the works. From December 1979, it was possible to travel wrong-line, as the down line was bi-directional from Burntisland East crossover to Colinswell.

The level crossing gates at the entrance to the works were under the control of British Aluminium staff, but BAC staff had to attend when trains were entering or leaving the site. There the rake was handed over to the internal railway. Thus, the train was provided with three methods of haulage in a couple of miles. The shuttle arrived from Thornton each morning, under the command of a class 'J37' or 'J38', later a class '20' diesel.

The locomotives, which operated on the Burntisland Aluminium Company system, were:

No.	Type	Date	Builder	Works No.	Remarks
Standard Gauge Steam					
1	0-4-0ST	1915	Peckett	1376	Sold to Lochty Railway, April 1973
2	0-4-0ST	1921	Peckett	1579	Sold to H.P. Bulmer, February 1972
3	0-4-0ST	1937	Andrew Barclay	2046	
Standard Gauge Diesel					
1	0-4-0	1949	John Fowler	4210004	Bought from United Fireclay in November 1971.
2	0-4-0	1951	John Fowler	4210045	Bought from United Fireclay in November 1971
2 ft gauge Diesel Mechanical					
1	0-4-0	1944	Ruston & Hornsby	223698	Scrapped at Thomas Muir, Thornton
2	0-4-0	1942	Ruston & Hornsby	217973	

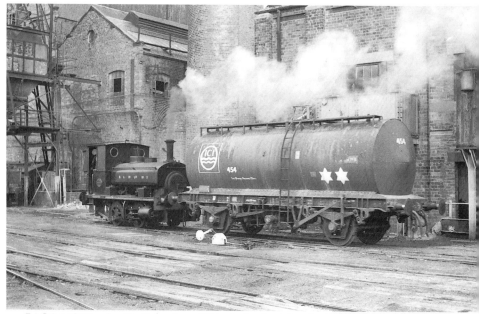

BAC 0-4-0ST Barclay No. 3 shunts an ICI tank of soda at the aluminium works, Burntisland on 24th April, 1971.   *Ken Falconer*

BAC 0-4-0ST Barclay No. 3, at 'The Bammie' on 4th December, 1967.   *Ken Falconer*

One of the BAC Peckett 0-4-0STs outside the shed on 11th December, 1968.   *Ken Falconer*

BAC 0-4-0ST Peckett No. 1, shunts a rake of 16 ton mineral wagons on 24th April, 1971.
Ken Falconer

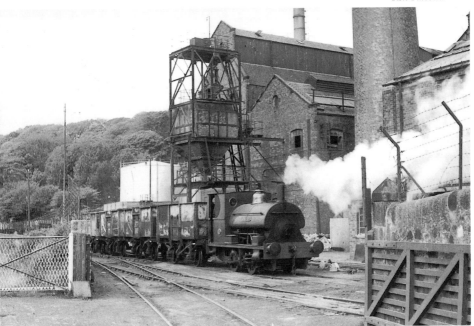

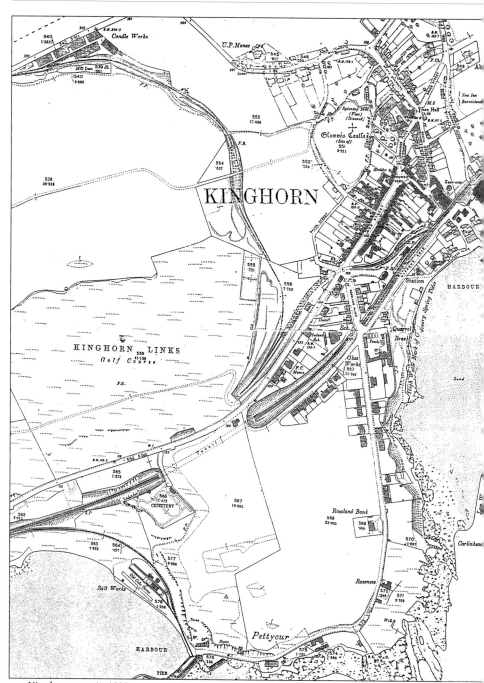

Kinghorn area in 1895.

Courtesy James Edmiston

The alumina for Ballachulish (for the Kinlockleven works) was uplifted in the evening by the final Thornton trip working of the day. This double shift was known locally as the 'Bammie' after the nickname for the works. A separate working took refined aluminium powder for Fort William to the west. The early evening train arrived usually with a consignment of coal from the Frances Colliery at Dysart or simply a guard's van. Travel was usually from Burntisland towards Glasgow via the Forth Bridge. At Cadder Yard to the east of Glasgow the train would be formed into the overnight goods to the West Highland line for delivery to the aluminium smelters based around Fort William

With around 500 employees at the turn of the 21st century, the aluminium works were the largest employer in Burntisland, surviving the reduction in the workforce at the railway, the harbour and the shipyard. The rail-connected sidings were cut in the 1980s.

The Kinghorn Branches

The branch was the last vestige of the line laid down to Pettycur pier to provide for supplies and access for new rolling stock for the Edinburgh & Northern Railway. Leaving the up main line on a trailing connection, the ⅓ mile-long branch maintained an incline of 1 in 28 falling on a steady curve to the pier, pretty steep by any measure. There was one passing loop below the halfway mark and a trailing branch into the bottle works. Coke ovens were sited alongside and served by this branch from 1870 to 1890. The railway also served salt pans. In 1908, the Kinghorn Bottle Company was created, and a skilled workforce was employed with many immigrants from Poland, Russia and Holland. By 1914, upwards of 100 employees, many more from Burntisland and Kirkcaldy worked at the bottle works which although rail connected did not operate its own locomotives. At its peak in 1965, 200 were employed there.

The bottle works was close to the pier and so was able to import raw materials - coal, soda ash and cullett (broken glass) - from its opening. Sand was dredged from the sandbanks off shore and used in the production of glass. However until April 1980, when production ceased, soda ash was brought to the site, initially by rail. This traffic was latterly operated by a diesel shunter on a trip working from Burntisland on a 'one engine in steam' basis. However, the Pettycur branch closed to traffic in 1968 and the material was brought by road.

An Edinburgh businessman, Graham Yule, saw a commercial opportunity in the sands to the west of Kinghorn and before the building of Rosyth Naval base, in 1901 laid a line of rails on the sand to the west of the Pettycur pier branch. A winding drum was installed next to the junction at the main line and at low water, men loaded small bogie wagons with sand from Pettycur Sands, which were then hauled to the level of the line before being transferred into rail wagons. Half a million tons of sand was thus removed and taken to Rosyth to be used in the creation of the harbour there. The work continued until 1937. A short branch also left the main line on the east of Kinghorn and provided access to the shipyard at Abden.

There were a number of waggonways and other private railways operating along the northern bank of the River Forth. Although not all of them were relevant to Burntisland, one or two will stand some scrutiny. In particular the early waggonways, which were established in the 18th century, add a further dimension to the rail traffic of Fife.

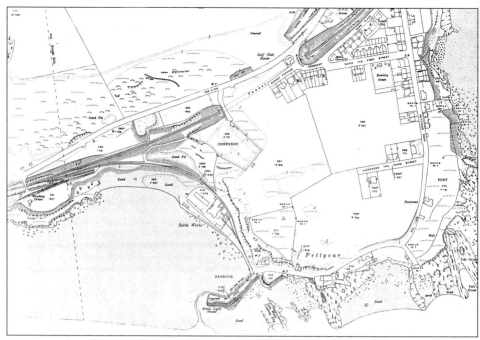

Pettycur branch in 1911, showing Bottleworks and winding drum.   *Courtesy James Edmiston*

Kinghorn bottle works in the early 1950s.   *James Edmiston*

Halbeath Waggonway and Colliery Railway

The Lloyd brothers, English merchants in Amsterdam and owners of the Halbeath Colliery, first promoted the Halbeath waggonway in 1781. The line, consisting of a 'waggon road laid with timber' five miles long from Halbeath Colliery to the Forth, was opened in 1783 and subsequently an office was opened at the harbour at Inverkeithing in 1790. Coal wagons, 24 in number, were used to bring coal down to the shore two tons at a time, drawn by one or sometimes two horses.

The system was relaid in 1811 with iron rails, permitting one horse to draw two 3 ton wagons making up to three journeys each day. A branch was added at the head of the line, at Guttergates near Halbeath, to the Townhill collieries, a few miles north-west near Dunfermline and 13 passing loops were created to allow for the increase of traffic in quarried stone from nearby. Several other collieries joined the system and when Halbeath Colliery ceased production in 1844, the railway was maintained.

On 10th June, 1846, Messrs Brown, Garden & Co., then lessees of the Halbeath Colliery, introduced a proposal to the Directors of the Edinburgh & Northern that the company construct a 'tram road' to connect the colliery with the intended branch line to Dunfermline. The lessees would pay interest on the cost of the junction over 13 years, any excess profits which the E&NR made from the link would be used to offset the interest. The arrangement was to be subject to conditions, namely the approval of Grainger (the E&NR's Engineer) and the signing of a petition in favour of the railway's Bill for a Dunfermline branch. The E&NR Board gave the proposal serious consideration and put the idea to an arbiter to decide the price to be paid, with a minimum of £15,000 and a maximum of £25,000.

In November 1846, discussions were opened with the Edinburgh & Perth Railway, which was about to make a speculative purchase of the Halbeath Colliery Railway (HCR) through its sponsors, the North British Railway. The E&PR saw the purchase as one way of preventing the E&NR claiming sole rights to the West Fife coalfield. A properly engineered route from Dunfermline to the Forth over the Halbeath system would deny much traffic to the Edinburgh & Northern Railway. The latter had reason to suspect that both the Scottish Central and Stirling & Dunfermline companies were in the background to the bidding, also in an attempt to court the coal owners of West Fife.

The E&NR increased its offer to £18,000, only to be told that it had been beaten by the NBR, which was prepared to sell the HCR to the Edinburgh & Northern for £25,000! Revenue on the colliery railway was less than £600 per annum after payment of leases. The Northern Board agreed that 'all idea of relieving the NBR of the purchase at the price asked be abandoned.' The E&PR persisted with its action and had a valuation of the HCR, the wagon fleet then totalling 45 with a nominal value of £10 each. The colliery railway was subsequently sold to the Edinburgh & Perth company and leased to local operators.

When the E&PR Bill failed (twice) and was withdrawn, the Northern Directors went ahead with their branch line to Dunfermline, strenuously opposed by the owners of the HCR, concerned that the flat crossing of the two lines would be dangerous. Amendments were made to allow the Dunfermline branch to pass over the Halbeath system and opposition was thereby removed. In the following year, 1847, the provisions of the Bill allowed for the HCR to pass over the railway, a situation which met once more with opposition from the E&PR. When the Railway Commissioner's surveyor reported that an entirely different crossing to any of the previous three be made, stalemate resulted. The lessees wanted a bridge over the line, while the owners wanted a bridge under the line.

The only option was to delay the E&NR's branch to Dunfermline by a further year and seek three Bills in the 1848 Parliamentary session, one for each possible option of crossing. All three proposals failed and, as the E&PR had also now lost any expectation of a line to Perth, an agreement was reached with Townhill Colliery owners, Thomas Spowart, to break their previous agreement and free the E&NR to construct the remaining link in its branch. The Townhill Colliery line was purchased at a total cost of £14,000.

On reviewing progress of the line, the Directors found that serious errors had been made in the levels and the permission of the Halbeath company would be required to proceed with the Dunfermline line. After negotiation, the obstacles were removed and the line completed.

Around a decade later, the Halbeath lines were extended further, westward to the Elgin system, bringing it to the Wellwood Colliery, also owned by Thomas Spowart. The line was discontinued in favour of the Elgin lines in 1867, when traffic was taken to the North British Railway port at Charlestown and coal exports from Inverkeithing ceased.

Townhill Colliery Company wagon.   *HMRS/R.Y. Pickering Collection W184*

Fordell Waggonway

Of the many waggon ways that brought coal from the West Fife coalfield, those that intersected the main lines around Burntisland were Fordell and Halbeath. Fordell was the earlier by only a few years, being laid down perhaps as early as 1752, but certainly by 1769. Coal had been worked from the estate for a couple of centuries before that and was carried by horse and pannier to Inverkeithing. The creation of a wooden waggonway meant that the proprietor of the mine was able to increase the tonnage carried to around 30,000 tons per annum. The 1769 line consisted of wooden rails on wooden sleepers and ran for four miles from Fordell to St David's harbour on the Forth, a few miles upstream from Burntisland.

In 1794, *The Original Statistical Account of Scotland* recorded that the line had double rails of beech over fir on wooden sleepers, spaced two feet apart. Three ton waggons were each drawn over the line by one or two horses, a total of 50 being employed. It was leased in 1798, although the line was in poor condition and would cost £470 per mile to replace as opposed to £125 for replacement of the single line alone. Renewal was recommended every five years.

Grainger and Miller produced a plan in 1828 to take the line to the west pier at St David's. In 1831/32, Robert Stevenson and Grainger and Miller offered an estimate for the new line but the colliery manager believed that it was too expensive. His plan was for malleable iron rails, using existing three-ton wagons. Newer wagons were considered to reduce haulage costs, as they would be 18 cwt tare as opposed to the 22 cwt of the older ones.

Robert Hawthorn produced a later plan in 1834, proposing 28 lb. malleable iron rails on 9 lb. cast chairs or stone setts together with larger wagons which would take between 2¾-3 tons of coal. He also suggested a new line to the harbour with three or four self-acting inclines each taking six wagons. The track was relayed in 1866 with second-hand rails from the North British Railway and the first locomotive was delivered from Hawthorn's in 1868. Later engines arrived in 1871 from Henry Hughes and Company and 1881 from Grant, Ritchie of Kilmarnock. The track gauge was 4 ft 4 in. with fish-bellied rails. The system operated until the 1950s.

Royal Navy Stores, Donibristle

A standard gauge railway was opened between Donibristle and Inverkeithing, independent of the NBR main line. The line was used to carry stores from the jetty at Inverkeithing to the aerodrome at Donibristle base. The locomotive first employed at the opening of the line was an Andrew Barclay 0-6-0T, works No. 1663, with 12 in. x 20 in. outside cylinders. This engine was believed to be the only one built to this design and was new for the line in April 1920. It was replaced in 1951 by a Barclay 0-4-0ST, (works No. 1387 of 1915), transferred from Rosyth Dockyard where it had been since new. The original engine was sold to a ship breaker at Rosyth in 1951 before moving to Faslane in 1955 and subsequently being returned and scrapped at Rosyth in 1963. The second locomotive only lasted until 1956 when it was sold for scrap to George Campbell of Airdrie. A further replacement was ordered from F.C. Hibberd and

Co. of Park Royal, in London and delivered in 1955. This was a four-wheel diesel mechanical locomotive (works No. 3740) which remained there until the depot closed in August 1959, when the diesel was transferred. This engine then became No. 3724 at Rosyth Dockyard.

One highlight of the later years at Donibristle, which was known in the Admiralty as HMS *Merlin*, was the arrival on 3rd March, 1946 of the Gresley 'A4' Pacific, No. 588 *Merlin*. The British Railways district superintendent, B.P. Blackburn, received a plaque from Captain C. Chatwin, commanding officer of HMS *Merlin*, the Royal Naval Air Station Donibristle, commemorating the association between the men of the depot and the locomotive. The 'A4', still in wartime black livery and wearing its 1946 number was brought into the depot from the East Coast main line over the works lines for the ceremony. Two brass plates enamelled with an illustration of a merlin in flight were attached to the locomotive. The locomotive driver, Bill Stevenson, and others in the party were then treated to an aircraft flight from Donibristle over the Forth and the hills of Perthshire.

Caldwell's Paper Mill Co. Ltd

Caldwell began making paper at Inverkeithing in 1893 and the company existed in various forms before becoming a subsidiary of the Inveresk Paper Company. The mill was situated to the south of the Rosyth branch line from Inverkeithing alongside the harbour, ideally situated for rail operations. It operated a number of locomotives in its works almost from the outset until it stopped using rail in 1972. Its first locomotive was named *Forward* and was purchased from the neighbouring firm of Thomas Ward in 1925. This was an 0-4-0T from Fletcher, Jennings which was built around 1889 at their Lowca Works in Whitehaven.

Caldwell & Company wagon.   *HMRS/ACP505*

Locomotives of the E&NR and EP&DR

R. & W. Hawthorn and Hawthorn's of Leith

The details of the E&NR locomotives are not clear, being further complicated by assembly of some engines at Leith. Hawthorn's of Leith ran a separate order book after 1846. The order book (1845-6) does not correspond directly with the believed delivery sequence.

No.	Type	Cyls (in.)	Driving wheels	Wheels	Works No	Delivered	NBR No.	Notes
1-2	0-4-2	15 x 21	5 ft 0 in.	3 ft 6 in.	494-5	8.1847	111, 112	
3-5	0-4-2	15 x 21	5 ft 0 in.	3 ft 6 in.	614-6	8.1847	113-115	Erected at Leith
6-8	0-4-2	15 x 21	5 ft 0 in.	3 ft 6 in.	499-501	9.1847	116-8	
9-12	0-6-0	16 x 24	4 ft 6 in.	-	610-3	1847-49	119-22	Erected at Leith
13	0-6-0	15 x 24	4 ft 6 in.	-	688	1847	123	
14-15	2-2-2	15 x 21	6 ft 0 in.	3 ft 0 in.	529-30	5.1848	124-5	Former MR order
16	2-2-2	15 x 21	6 ft 0 in.	3 ft 0 in.	676	1848	126	
17	2-2-2	15 x 21	6 ft 0 in.	3 ft 0 in.	617	1848	127	Erected at Leith
18	0-6-0	15 x 24	4 ft 6 in.	-	677	1848	128	
19-20	0-4-2	15 x 21	5 ft 0 in.	3 ft 6 in.	566-7	1.1848	129-30	
21-22	0-6-0	15 x 24	4 ft 6 in.	-	678-9	9.1848	131-2	Erected at Leith
23-24	0-6-0	15 x 24	4 ft 6 in.	-	681, 680	1848	133-4	Erected at Leith
25-26	0-4-2	15 x 21	5 ft 0 in.	?	673-4	1849	135-6	Erected at Leith
27	0-6-0	16 x 24	5 ft 0 in.	-	596	1850	137	
28-29	0-6-0	18 x 24	5 ft 0 in.	-	727-8	1851	138-9	
30	0-4-0	13 x 16	4 ft 0 in.	-		1847	140	Built at Leith. Granton line
31	0-4-2	13 x 20	4 ft 6 in.	3 ft 0 in.		1845	141	Built at Leith. Granton line
32	0-4-0	13 x 16	4 ft 0 in.	-		1847	142	Built at Leith. Granton line
33-34	2-4-0T	14 x 20	5 ft 6 in.	?		1850	143-4	
35	0-6-0	16 x 22	5 ft 0 in.	-		1856		See No. 35 EP&DR
36	0-4-0	13 x 16	3 ft 10 in.	-		1847	146	
39	0-4-0	13 x 16	4 ft 0 in.	-		1847	149	
41-42	2-2-0	13 x 16	4 ft 0 in.	-		1847	151-2	
43	0-4-0	14 x 18	4 ft 6 in.	-	132	12.1855	153	Built at Leith. Granton line
44-45	0-6-0	16 x 14	5 ft 0 in.	-		1861	154-5	Built at Leith
47	0-4-0	14 x 18	4 ft 6 in.	-		2.1861	157	Leslie Rly, operated by EP&DR
48	0-4-0	14 x 18	4 ft 6 in.	-		1860	158	Kinross Rly, operated by EP&DR

George Dow (*The First Railway Across the Border*) records that NBR 0-4-2s Nos. 5-14 were originally intended for the Edinburgh & Northern Railway but were purchased from R. & W. Hawthorn by the NBR at a cost of £1,650 each. He also record that the Edinburgh, Perth and Dundee Railway purchased the following R. & W. Hawthorn locomotives from the NBR. They were rebuilt with 16 in. x 24 in. cylinders.

21	0-6-0	15 x 24	4 ft 3 in.	476	1846	29	Bought 1860
22	0-6-0	15 x 24	4 ft 3 in.	478	1846	31	Bought 1856
23	0-6-0	15 x 24	4 ft 3 in.	479	1846	32	Bought 1856

Neilson & Co.

38, 46	0-6-0	16 x 24	5 ft 0 in.	673-674	1861	148, 156	

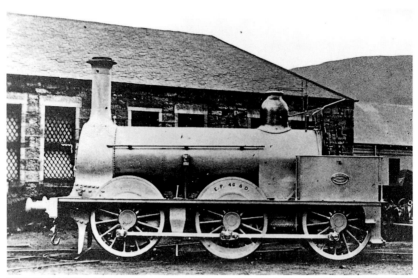

EP&DR 0-6-0 No. 46.   *James F. McEwan Collection/T25/15/1351*

Edinburgh, Perth & Dundee Railway, Burntisland Works

The workshops at Burntisland were used for repairs to these unreliable early locomotives. It was not unknown for some to be completely rebuilt from the frames up, thus ensuring that the work was charged to revenue account and not to capital. One such engine was No. 41, a 2-2-2 rebuilt as an 0-4-0 which became NBR No. 151. Building of new engines at the workshops in Burntisland is believed to have begun in 1861 when Robert Nicholson built a 2-2-2 inside-framed express passenger engine. This was followed by a further four 0-6-0 locomotives during the next two years.

No.		Type	Cylinders (in.)	Driving wheels	Wheels	Date	NBR No.	Notes
37	*Oakley*	2-2-2	15 x 20	6 ft 0 in.	?	1861	147	built to Nicholson's design
40		0-6-0	16 x 24	5 ft 0 in.	-	11.1861	150	
35		0-6-0	16 x 24	5 ft 0 in.	-	1.1862	145	
49		0-6-0	16 x 24	5 ft 0 in.	-	1862	159	completed by NBR
50		0-6-0	16 x 24	5 ft 0 in.	-	1863	160	completed by NBR

The Burntisland built engines lasted well into NBR days, the final one to be scrapped was NBR No. 159, never being entirely rebuilt. With Wheatley's plain chimney and Holmes' safety valves, she lasted until 1896.

Coal Shipments through Burntisland

Tonnage by Colliery shipped through Burntisland, Methil and other ports
52 weeks to 31st January, 1905

This is not a complete list of collieries in Fife at that time. It does, however, show the emphasis location had on the choice of port for shipment. The farther east, the more likely Methil will be used, the farther west, Burntisland is the choice. Those collieries in mid-Fife could, and often did, select either or both ports. Burntisland's dependence on Fife Coal Company, as the largest shipper with 60 per cent of tonnage shown, is clear.

Company	Colliery	Station	Burntisland	Methil	Other	Colliery Total	Company Total
Balgonie Coal Co.	Balgonie	Thornton	27,042	73,815	202	100,429	100,429
Bowhill Coal Co.	Bowhill	Cardenden	118,514	91,541	16,342	266,397	266,397
Bowman & Co.	Denbeath	Methil	nil	90,399	nil	90,399	319,376 (Burntisland 5,176)
	Isabella	Buckhaven	1,379	64,937	nil	66,316	
	Muiredge	Buckhaven	1,333	75,991	802	78,126	
	Rosie	Buckhaven	2,464	81,944	127	84,535	
Carden Coal Co.	Cardenden	Cardenden	539	8,568	18	9,125	9,125
Coltness Iron Co.	Blairhall	East Grange	8,925	5,041	1,171	15,137	15,137
Dundonald Collieries	Dundonald	Cardenden	16,246	12,767	893	29,906	29,906
Donibristle Coal Co.	Donibristle	Cowdenbeath Old	27,857	12,237	12,990	53,084	53,084
Fife Coal Co.	Aitken	Kelty	145,398	46,227	41,926	233,551	1,713,619 (Burntisland 689,395)
	Benarty	Kelty	8,868	5,104	55,387	69,359	
	Blairadam	Kelty	21,629	5,792	nil	27,421	
	Blairenbathie	Kelty	24,789	7,338	nil	32,127	
	Cowdenbeath	Cowdenbeath	170,704	160,870	2,313	333,887	
	Foulford	Cowdenbeath	63,556	88,816	335	152,707	
	Kinnaird	Kelty	13,644	6,831	7,334	27,809	
	Leven Nos. 1 & 3	Methil	nil	258,411	nil	258,411	
	Lindsay	Kelty	45,679	20,067	5,009	70,755	
	Lumphinnans	Cowdenbeath Old	44,109	37,772	520	82,401	
	Lumphinnans North	Kelty	106, 103	34,119	50,636	273,259	
	Mossbeath	Cowdenbeath	42,879	19,868	658	63,405	
	Wellsgreen	Wemyss Castle	2,037	168,706	177	170,920	
R. Forrester & Co.	Craigend	Kelty	1,451	6,498	2,186	10,135	10,135
Walter Herd & Sons Ltd	Dunnikier	Sinclairtown	25,753	34,753	84	60,590	60,590
Henderson's Trustees	Fordell	Crossgates	239	105	2,778	3,122	3,122
J. McKelvick & Co.	Balcarries	Largoward	1,123	3,859	925	5,907	5,907
John Nimmo & Sons	Rosebank	Whitemyre Jn	23,635	22,857	318	46,810	46,810
Henry Ness & Co.	Muirbeath	Townhill Jn	8,498	19,602	76	28,176	33,072 (Burntisland 10,615)
	Muircockhall	Townhill Jn	2,117	2,718	61	4,896	
Oakley Collieries Ltd	Oakley	Oakley	20,150	28,694	3,712	52,556	52,556
Earl of Rosslyn's Collieries	Randolph	Thornton	21,773	34,219	26	56,018	56,018
Rosewell Gas Coal Co.	Lassodie Mill	Kelty	5,473	6,261	nil	11,734	11,734
Wilsons and Clyde Coal Co.	Glencraig	Cardenden	57,152	73,614	107,671	238,437	238,437
Thomas Spowart & Co.	Arthur	Whitemyre Jn	4,840	1,594	380	6,814	100,872 (Burntisland 70,866)
	Elgin & Wellwood	Townhill	12,202	2,786	1,038	16,026	
	Lassodie	Kelty	53,708	17,592	6,335	77,635	
	Lochend	Steelend	186	171	nil	307	
Wemyss Coal Co.	Lochhead	Wemyss Castle	580	4,266	4	4,850	343,718 (Burntisland 580)
	Michael	Wemyss Castle	nil	13,018	54	13,072	
	Wemyss Collieries	Wemyss Private Railway	nil	325,796		325,796	
West of Fife Coal Co.	Saline	Steelend	5,470	7,815	416	13,701	28,874 (Burntisland 15,235)
	Townhill	Townhill	9,765	2,774	2,634	15,173	
Total			1,147,739	1,986,158	325,538	3,459,435	

Source: Parliamentary Evidence given to support the Buckhaven Dock Bill of 1907

Tonnage exported from Burntisland between 1877 to 1912 compared with Methil and total tonnage mined in Fife

The growth of Methil as competition to Burntisland can be seen, with the former achieving one million tons by 1897. The opening of the East dock brought about a sharp rise in Burntisland's tonnage in 1902 but the town never regained its early dominance.

Year	Burntisland	Methil	Fife	Year	Burntisland	Methil	Fife
1877	288,919		1,308,651	1895	762,815	727,680	3,911,235
1878	355,505		1,676,901	1896	787,184	857,892	3,633,455
1879	470,639		1,726,701	1897	886,936	1,090,324	4,077,818
1880	451,830		1,930,511	1898	916,301	1,230,554	4,447,569
1881	626,830		2,023,801	1899	879,718	1,316,937	4,927,489
1882	665,129		2,052,732	1900	983,588	1,685,628	5,419,373
1883	749,852		2,174,555	1901	986,057	1,574,896	5,601,501
1884	704,689		2,114,588	1902	1,524,207	1,759,041	6,134,171
1885	772,967		2,291,509	1903	1,513,016	1,792,078	6,376,985
1886	806,232		2,295,926	1904	1,598,021	1,985,826	6,586,154
1887	724,402	219,884	2,585,412	1905	1,817,263	2,423,372	7,241,439
1888	652,514	410,131	2,459,395	1906	2,013,454	2,793,257	7,783,459
1889	739,306	556,840	2,761,616	1907	2,182,144	2,823,720	8,530,043
1890	667,997	666,403	3,121,646	1908	2,164,293	2,559,500	8,412,856
1891	703,608	781,805	3,301,000	1909	2,194,608	2,691,109	8,425,785
1892	771,824	810,545	3,573,818	1910	2,182,293	2,926,210	8,647,404
1893	772,056	823,305	3,619,550	1911	2,430,708	3,012,440	9,037,790
1894	480,712	527,564	2,784,019	1912	2,328,456	2,557,245	n/a

Source: *Mining in the Kingdom of Fife* A.S. Cunningham 1907

Tonnage Exported from 1891 to 1902

	1898	1899	1900	1901	1902
Germany	361,000	348,000	346,500	359,500	433,500
Sweden	193,500	215,500	268,500	245,500	421,000
Russia	55,500	18,500	38,000	25,000	115,000
Denmark	145,000	142,000	161,500	157,500	198,500
Norway	42,500	53,000	62,000	40,500	43,500
France	14,000	14,000	35,500	25,500	54,000
Mediterranean	16,000	7,000	28,500	11,000	29,000
Total	828,000	799,000	895,500	864,500	1,294,173

The biggest customers for Fife coal in Sweden and Denmark were the state railways.

Ferry Revenue
1835 to 1838

Showing the relative number of crossings by passengers and freight to the Fife coast from Midlothian. Burntisland was the favourite destination for passenger traffic, but the Pettycur and Kirkcaldy passages generated more revenue by attracting more first class passengers. Revenue for goods and freight, including carriages, reveals that Pettycur and Kirkcaldy also had the edge over Burntisland. All that was about to change with the arrival of the railway.

Year	Crossing	Number of Paying Passengers		Revenue from Fares and Freight			Average of freight per passage		
		Passages made	Revenue	Passengers	Goods	Total	£	s.	d.
		£	£	£	£	£			
1835	Burntisland	2,274	4,851	1,224	75	1,299		11	5
	Pettycur	1,688	8,274	2,412	208	2,620	1	11	5
	Kirkcaldy	1,489	9,735	2,470	78	2,548	1	14	3
Total 52 weeks		5,451	2,860	6,106	361	6,467	1	3	9
1836	Burntisland	2,155	1,4324	1,180	53	1,233		11	5
	Pettycur	1,637	26,829	2,285	195	2,479	1	10	3
	Kirkcaldy	1,467	29,564	2,450	92	2,541	1	14	8
Total 52 weeks		5,259	70,717	5,915	340	6,255	1	3	10
1837	Burntisland	2,095	15,252	1,247	53	1,300		12	5
	Pettycur	1,566	20,837	1,771	175	1,946	1	4	10
	Kirkcaldy	1,357	27,574	2,304	49	2,353	1	14	8
Total 46 weeks *		5,018	63,663	5,322	277	5,599	1	2	3
1837	Burntisland	207	1,162	64	3	67		6	6
	Pettycur	219	3,290	202	19	221	1	0	2
Total 6 weeks		426	4,452	266	22	288		13	6
1838	Burntisland	2,224	19,319	1,091	37	1,128		10	2
	Pettycur	2,999	23,637	1,417	196	1,613		10	9
	Kirkcaldy*	143	2,594	151	7	158	1	2	2
Total 52 weeks		5,366	45,550	2,660	240	2,900		10	10

* The ferry trustees' boats ceased plying to Kirkcaldy from 11th November, 1837 to 11th November, 1838.

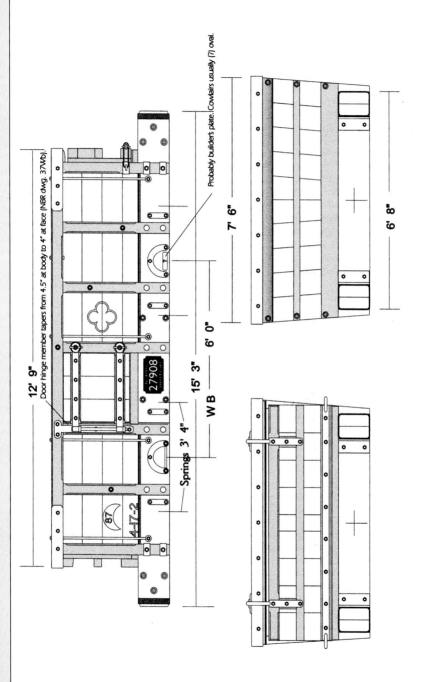

12' 9"

Door hinge member tapers from 4.5' at body to 4" at face (NBR dwg. 37Vb).

7' 6"

6' 0"

15' 3"

W B

Springs 3' 4"

87

4-17-2

27908

Probably builder's plate. Cowlairs usually (?) oval.

6' 8"

North British Railway, 7/8T Mineral Wagon #27908. Drawing derived from George Washington Wilson Archive C1398

Note that the end door has vertical sides and may be a replacement.

Mineral Wagons Observed at Burntisland in 1880

Richard Davidson has produced scaled drawings of several of the 19th century mineral wagons photographed at the dockside in Burntisland. The photograph has not been reproduced in this book as it is amongst the best known images of Burntisland docks and can be found in many illustrated books, amongst the best known is *George Washington Wilson and the Scottish Railways* where it may be seen on page 20. These are some of Richard's observations.

NBR 8 ton mineral wagons Nos. 27908 & 32855. Outside frames with dumb buffers with side and end doors. The latter would allow discharge into ships.

DCC 8 ton mineral wagon No 52. Similar design to NBR end door only. Possibly Dundonald Collieries Company [or maybe Donibristle Coal Company, author]. The body colour is very light, possibly light grey.

RCC 8 ton mineral wagon No. 25. Similar design to NBR end door only. Possibly Rosewell Gas Coal Company. The body colour is dark, possibly black or dark red.

Lochgelly Iron and Coal Company wagon of uncertain capacity No. 617. Dumb buffers with end door only. Body colour, medium red with white band and (presumably) black lettering.

Lochgelly Iron and Coal Company unknown load, tare and number. Outside framing and dumb buffers with end door only. Colour as previous Lochgelly wagon.

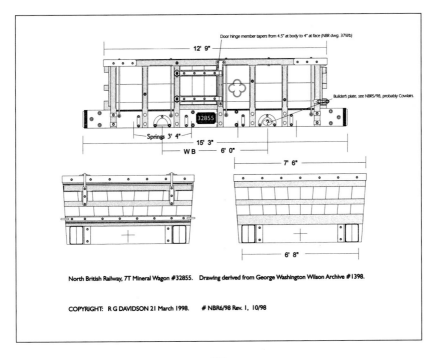

North British Railway, 7T Mineral Wagon #32855. Drawing derived from George Washington Wilson Archive #1398.

COPYRIGHT: R G DAVIDSON 21 March 1998.   # NBR6/98 Rev. 1, 10/98

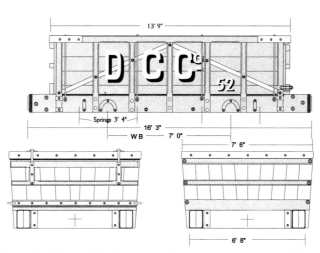

Data derived from GWW photo C1423x. End views based on NBR standard wagon layout as in drawing No. 37Wb. Plank spacing of side conjectural, based on similar size CR wagon (OPC 3G/W/8059).   Lettering approximate in style and placement

COPYRIGHT; R G DAVIDSON 1999.   Drawing No. PO(S)/10/99

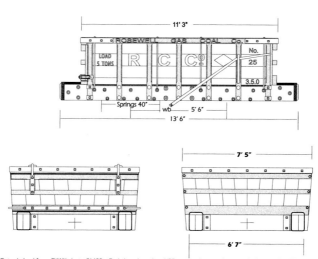

Data derived from GWW photo C1423x. End views based on NBR standard wagon layout as in drawing No. 37Wb. Plank spacing of side conjectural.   Lettering approximate in style and placement

COPYRIGHT; R G DAVIDSON 1999.   Drawing No. PO(S)/11/99. Rev. 2; June 1999

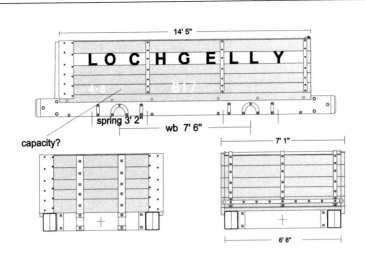

Details from GWW print C1423x, Burntisland ~1880.

COPYRIGHT: R.G.DAVIDSON 1999. Drawing No. PO(S) 12/99

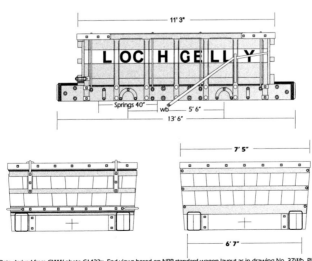

Data derived from GWW photo C1423x. End views based on NBR standard wagon layout as in drawing No. 37Wb. Plank spacing of side conjectural. Lettering approximate in style and placement

COPYRIGHT; R G DAVIDSON 1999. Drawing No. PO(S)/13/99

Appendix Five

Boats on the Burntisland Crossing

Passenger Ferries

PS *Comet* (1834) ? tons Wooden paddles, 135 ft 9 in. x 16 ft 7 in. x 9 ft 0 in. Built at Rotherhithe, Surrey. Purchased from Miller and Ravenhill of Blackwall, in 1848 by E&NR; to EP&DR 1st August, 1849. Operated Granton-Burntisland ferry from 1848-1850 and usually on Tay Ferry from 1850-1852. Sold to J. & M. Anderson, ferry operators, 1852.

PS *Maid of Leven* (1839) 76 gross tons. Wood paddles. 123 ft 3 in. x 19 ft 0 in. x 9 ft 0 in. Built at Paisley for Dumbarton Steamboat Co. 1844. Sold to John Gladstone and operated ferry 1844-1853 chartered to E&NR then EP&DR from 1st January, 1847 to 19th July, 1853. Operated on Tay service during 1849. Sold by Gladstone to C. Watson, Middlesborough 1853.

PS *Granton* (1844) 196 gross tons. Iron paddles. 120 ft 0 in. x 20 ft 0 in. x 9 ft 0 in. Built at Leith by John Maxton & Co. Engines two-cylinder simple by builders. Built for John Gladstone and Duke of Buccleuch. Taken over by E&NR 1st January, 1847 then by EP&DR 1st August, 1849. Sold to R. Cook and J. Inkster 1856. Coal hulk at Leith, July 1886.

PS *Burntisland* (1844) 196 gross tons. Iron paddles. 120 ft 0 in. x 20 ft 0 in. x 9 ft 0 in. Built at Leith by John Maxton & Co. Engines two-cylinder simple by builders. Built for John Gladstone and Duke of Buccleuch. Taken over by E&NR 1st January, 1847 then by EP&DR 1st August, 1849. Worked on Tay service for a time in 1849. Sold to J. Bremner, Liverpool 1851.

PS *Forth* (1846) 210 gross tons. Iron paddles. 144 ft 5 in. x 26 ft 10 in. x 10 ft 5 in. Built by Hawarden Iron Co., Hawarden, Flintshire. Engines two-cylinder simple by builders. Originally ordered by John Gladstone. Taken over by the E&NR February 1847 then by EP&DR 1st August, 1849 and by North British Railway Company on 1st August, 1862. Saloon fitted to after deck February 1858. Sank Burntisland 27th September, 1863 but refloated. Collided with PS *Kinloch* on 21st November, 1872 when backing out of Granton. Sold for £725 to S. & H. Morton, Leith 1879.

PS *Thane of Fife* (1847) 171 gross tons. Iron paddles. 141 ft 0 in. x 10 ft 3 in. x 9 ft 8 in. Built at Blackwall, London by Miller and Ravenhill. Engines two-cylinder simple by builders. Built for E&NR 1848; to EP&DR 1st August, 1849 and the NBR 1st August, 1862. Usually on Tay Ferry service 1853-1879 but worked from Granton-Burntisland on occasions. Transferred to Queensferry Passage from September 1879 until 1890. Sold for £1,000 to P. & W. MacLellan, Glasgow 11th November, 1890.

PS *Auld Reekie* (1847) 163 gross tons. Iron paddles. 141 ft 6 in. x 19 ft 1 in. x 9 ft 1 in. Built at Blackwall, London by Miller and Ravenhill. Engines two-cylinder simple by Builders. Built for E&NR and in service from January 1848; to EP&DR 1st August, 1849 and to NBR 1st August, 1862. Operated on Granton-Burntisland ferry from 1848 to 1880 when saloon fitted for use on Tay Ferry until 1890. Sold for £1,000 to P. & W. MacLellan, Glasgow 11th November, 1890.

PS *Express* (1848) 269 gross tons. Iron paddles. 153 ft 0 in. x 24 ft 1 in. x 9 ft 9 in. Built at Blackwall, London by Miller and Ravenhill. Engines two-cylinder simple by builders. Built for E&NR, in service from 1st January, 1849. To EP&DR 1st August, 1849 and to NBR 1st August, 1862. Operated on the Tay Ferry service 1848-1875 then relegated to spare duties. Sold to John Key and Sons for breaking up in 1878 for the sum of £400.

PS *John Stirling* (1876) 427 gross tons. Iron paddles. 190 ft 3 in. x 27 ft 0 in. x 10 ft 6 in. Built at Kinghorn, Fife by J. Key & Sons. Engines two-cylinder simple by builders at Whitebank works, Kirkcaldy. Built for NBR and in service from 8th May, 1876. Required £2,000 of rock blasting at Burntisland to accommodate her draught. Sold 8th June, 1892 to T.C. Glover a civil engineer of Edinburgh with links to S. & H. Morton, shipbuilders of Leith.

PS *William Muir* (1879) 364 gross tons. Iron paddles. 174 ft 1 in. x 24 ft 1 in. x 10 ft 8 in. Built at Kinghorn, Fife by J. Key & Sons. Engines two-cylinder simple by builders at Whitebank works, Kirkcaldy with boilers originally for PS *Express*. Built for NBR transferred to LNER on 1st January, 1923. Rebuilt in 1910 when the fore-funnel and the forward boiler room were removed. Served as a minesweeper mainly based on Sheerness from 8th June, 1917 until 21st May 1919. Returned to Granton-Burntisland crossing on 16th July, 1919 after speedy refit. Withdrawn 2nd March, 1937. Taken to Charleston on 4th March to be broken up.

TSS *Thane of Fife* Built in 1910 by Cammel, Laird & Co. of Birkenhead as *Snowdrop* for Wallasey Corporation Ferries. 152 ft 3 in. x 38 ft 7 in. x 10 ft 11 in. Two three-cylinder engines. Served on Liverpool to New Brighton crossing. Transferred to LNER and renamed, modified at Grangemouth in October 1936 to provide room for motor vehicles. Withdrawn 1939 and requisitioned as naval tender. Broken up at Alloa in 1947.

Goods Ferries

PS *Leviathan* (1848) 399 gross tons. Iron paddles. 167 ft 8 in. x 34 ft 7 in. x 8 ft 6 in. Built at Govan, Glasgow by Robert Napier & Sons. Engines two steeple each of one cylinder by Builders. Built as a train ferry of 20-wagon capacity for EP&DR. To NBR 1st August, 1862. Repaired November 1878 by Ramage and Ferguson for £2,100. Sold to P. & W. MacLellan, Glasgow 18th September, 1890.

PS *Robert Napier* (1850) 243 gross tons. Iron paddles. 129 ft 7 in. x 23 ft 9 in. x 8 ft 6 in. Built at Govan, Glasgow by Robert Napier & Sons. Engines two-cylinder simple by Builders. Built as a train ferry of 20-wagon capacity for EP&DR. To NBR 1st August, 1862. Tonnage recalculated in 1876 to 216 gt and boat remeasured at 137 ft 5 in. x 24 ft 5 in. x 8 ft 6 in. Operated on Tayport-Broughty Ferry from 1851 to 1853 and from 1868 to 1880, on Granton-Burntisland route during remaining time. Sold for scrapping 1888.

PS *Carrier* (1858) 243 gross tons. Iron paddles. 124 ft 5 in. x 24 ft 8 in. x 9 ft 6 in. Built at Greenock by Scott & Co. Engines two-cylinder simple by Greenock Foundry Co. Built as a train ferry of 30-wagon capacity, for EP& DR. To NBR 1st August, 1862. Operated on Tayport-Broughty Ferry from 1858 to 1878 then on Granton-Burntisland Ferry after opening of the first Tay Bridge on 1st June, 1878. Sold to S. Mason, Edinburgh 1881.

PS *Balbirnie* (1861) 533 gross tons. Iron paddles. 199 ft 6 in. x 40 ft 5 in. x 8 ft 11 in. Built at Leith by S. & H. Morton. Engines two simple diagonal by builders. Built as a train ferry of 30-wagon capacity, for EP&DR. To NBR 1st August, 1862. Sold for £1,575 to P. & W. MacLellan, Glasgow 11th November, 1890.

PS *Kinloch* (1865) 585 gross tons. Iron paddles. 216 ft 0 in. x 36 ft 3 in. x 8 ft 0 in. Built at Glasgow by A & J Inglis. Engines two simple diagonal by builders. Built as a train ferry, 30-wagon capacity, for NBR Co. Sold for £1,875 to P. & W. MacLellan, Glasgow 11th November, 1890.

PS *Midlothian* (1881) 920 gross tons. Steel paddles. 262 ft 7 in. x 40 ft 3 in. x 10 ft 0 in. Built at Leith by Ramage & Ferguson. Engines compound diagonal two-cylinder by builders. Re-engined by John Key of Whitebank engineering works, Kirkcaldy. Built as a train ferry of 40-wagon capacity, for NBR. Sold for £6,750 to P. & W. MacLellan, Glasgow 11th November, 1890.

Post-War Ferries

MV *Bonnie Prince Charles* (1942) 460 gross tons. Twin screw, 180 ft x 38 ft. Built in Glasgow by P. & W. MacLellan. Two 12-cylinder Davey Paxman diesel engines. Purchased 1950 by John Hall Shipping Ltd, then to Forth Ferries Ltd. Sold 1954.

MV *Eriskay* (1943) 460 gross tons. Twin screw, 180 ft x 38 ft. Built in Glasgow by P. & W. MacLellan. Two 12-cylinder Davey Paxman diesel engines. Purchased 1950 by John Hall Shipping Ltd, then to Forth Ferries Ltd. Sold to India 1954.

MV *Flora Macdonald* (1942) 460 gross tons. Twin screw, 180 ft x 38 ft. Built in Glasgow by P. & W. MacLellan. Two 12-cylinder Davey Paxman diesel engines. Purchased 1950 by John Hall Shipping Ltd, then to Forth Ferries Ltd. Sold to India 1954.

MV *Glenfinnan* (1944) 460 gross tons. Twin screw, 180 ft x 38 ft. Built in Glasgow by P. & W. MacLellan. Two 12-cylinder Davey Paxman diesel engines. Purchased 1950 by John Hall Shipping Ltd, then to Forth Ferries Ltd. Sold to India 1954, lost 1955.

MV *Glenfinnan*, the ex-tank landing craft operating on the Forth on 10th July, 1952.
Douglas Yuill Collection

Appendix Six

Chronology

1836	13th August	Act for Edinburgh, Leith & Newhaven Railway
1842	31st August	Completion of extension to Trinity pier
1844	7th November	Committee of management for Edinburgh & Northern Railway set up
1845	31st July	Edinburgh & Northern Railway Act receives Royal Assent
	13th August	Initial Board meeting
	22nd November	Locomotives ordered from Hawthorn
1846	19th February	Completion of extension to Granton
	10th June	Halbeath waggonway offered to E&NR
	18th June	North British Railway opens
1847	7th August	Edinburgh, Leith & Granton Railway amalgamated with E&NR.
	3rd September	Inspection of the line
	17th September	Opening ceremony
	20th September	First public services
1848	18th July	Line opened to Perth
	September	Branch opened from Thornton to Crossgates
1849	13th January	Thomas Bouch joins the company as Manager
	April	Company re-incorporated as Edinburgh, Perth & Dundee Railway.
	13th December	Dunfermline branch opens fully.
1850	January	Trials of Bouch's Floating Railway at Burntisland
	March	PS *Leviathan* enters revenue service
	28th August	Stirling & Dunfermline Railway opens from Alloa
	1st October	Initial complaints about shortage of wagons for coalmasters
1851	April	Bouch resigns as Manager
1861	June	First extension of Burntisland harbour completed
1862	1st August	Edinburgh, Perth & Dundee Railway incorporated into North British Railway
1866	14th June	Launch of raft for construction of Forth Bridge
	3rd August	Work on Forth Bridge stopped
1872	5th November	NBR enters agreement with Burntisland to construct new dock
1876	8th May	PS *John Stirling* enters service
	1st December	West dock opens
1877	1st November	Dunfermline to North Queensferry branch opens
1878	31st May	Tay Bridge opens
1879	October	PS *William Muir* enters service
	28th December	Tay Bridge falls
1881	November	Harbour vested in commissioners
1887	20th April	New Tay Bridge opens
	April	First trains use Binnend Oil Company branch from Kinghorn
1890	4th March	Forth Bridge opens with lines to Burntisland and Cowdenbeath
	5th March	North Queensferry pier branch passenger services end
	Autumn	Six Forth ferries sold to P. & W. MacLellan
1896	3rd March	Auchtertool line opens

	July	New Act to build East dock
	9th December	Accident at Burntisland East
1910	15th January	PS *William Muir* undergoes rebuild
1914	14th April	Accident at Burntisland Junction, NBR Atlantic, 872 *Auld Reekie*, collides with goods train.
	1st October	Burntisland District Control instituted
	Autumn	Burntisland station destroyed by fire
1917		British Aluminium Company works opened
1918	25th June	Keel of first ship laid at Burntisland Shipbuilding yard
1936	26th April	Burntisland Junction signal box closed, East box renamed Burntisland Junction
1937	2nd March	PS *William Muir* concludes 57 years service
1940		Ferry crossing suspended during World War II
1951	1st May	New ferry service introduced with former tank landing craft
1970	1st February	District Control transferred from Burntisland to Edinburgh
1979	12th December	Burntisland East box closed
1989	May	New class 150 dmus enter service
1998	8th July	MGR Coal train derailed at Burntisland
2001	Summer	Burntisland station refurbished

The frame of the demolished Roundhouse in 1961.   *James F. McEwan/N3787*

Acknowledgements

As always with a book like this, there are a number of people who have offered help, freely given, and without whom the knowledge gathered would be incomplete. I express my sincere thanks to Richard Hollingworth for his encouragement and help, Alan Simpson for his exhaustive research, Iain Sommerville for history of Burntisland from his web site and Alex McInnes for details on Granton. Thanks also go to Don Martin, at East Dunbartonshire Libraries, for access to material from the late James McEwan. Illustrations from the collections of Douglas Yuill, Ken Falconer, Bill Lynn, Hamish Stevenson, Edward Wilson and James Edmiston, OBE enhance the text.

As ever, the National Archive of Scotland, West Register House was the essential primary source of railway history and additional material was found in Dunfermline Local History library. My thanks to the staff of both establishments and to St Andrews University Library and Kirkcaldy Museum for illustrations, and the National Library of Scotland Map Library.

Membership of the North British Railway Study Group is essential for research into this great Scottish railway. The NBR Study Group publishes a regular journal and readers interested in joining should contact the Membership Secretary, Bill Lynn, 2 Brecken Court, Saltwell Road South, Low Fell, GATESHEAD, NE9 6EY.

NBR point lever at Burntisland dock. *James F. McEwan/N3321*

Bibliography

Bradshaw's Railway Manual, David & Charles Reprint, 1969
Crossing the Forth, Hugh Douglas, Robert Hale, 1964
Early Scottish Colliery Waggonways, George Dott, St Margaret's Technical Press, 1947
Ferries in Scotland, Marie Weir, John Donald, 1988
Fife The Mining Kingdom, Guthrie Hutton, Stenlake, 1999
George Washington Wilson and the Scottish Railways, Durie and Mellor, Aberdeen University Library, 1983
Glimpses of Modern Burntisland, ex Baillie Erskine, The Fife Free Press, 1930
Industrial Locomotives of Scotland, Industrial Railway Society, 1976
Kinghorn Industries since 1790, Kinghorn Historical Society, 1993
Locomotive and Train Working in the Nineteenth Century, Volume Three, E.L. Ahrons, W. Heffer, 1952
Locomotives of the NBR, 1846-1882, The Stephenson Locomotive Society, 1970
Mining in the Kingdom of Fife, Andrew S. Cunningham, Dunfermline Press, 1913
Oil on the Rails, Allan Coppin, HMRS, 1999
Old Burntisland, Rhona Wilson, Stenlake, 1998
Old Kinghorn, Eric Eunson, Stenlake, 1998
Regional History of the Railways of Great Britain, Volume 15, Thomas and Thurnock, David & Charles, 1989
Scottish Locomotive History 1831-1923, Campbell Highet, George Allen and Unwin, 1970
St Andrews and Fife, Durie and Ingram, Aberdeen University Library, 1994
Steamers on the Forth, Ian Brodie, David & Charles, 1976
The Binnend Oilworks, Walter M. Stephen, Private publication, (? date)
The Fife Coal Company, Augustus Muir, Private publication, 1952
The Fordell Railway, J.E. & F. Inglis, Larbert, 1947
The Forth Railway Bridge, Anthony Murray, Mainstream, 1983
The Great Road between Forth and Tay, G.P. Bennett, Markinch Printing Company, (undated)
The North British Atlantics, John Thomas, David & Charles, 1972
The North British Railway, C. Hamilton Ellis, Ian Allan, 1955
The North British Railway, Volume I, John Thomas, David & Charles, 1969
The North British Railway, Volume II, John Thomas, David & Charles, 1975
The Origins of the Scottish Railway System, C.J.A. Robertson, John Donald, 1983
The Railway Mania and its Aftermath, Henry Lewin, David & Charles Reprint, 1968
The Railways of Fife, W.S. Bruce, Melven Press, 1980
The Railway Race to the North, O.S. Nock, Ian Allan, 1958
The Wemyss Private Railway, A.W. Brotchie, Oakwood Press, 1998
Fife Free Press
Fifeshire Advertiser
LNER Programme of Excursions and Special Trains, 1936
North British Railway Study Group *Journal*
Railway Magazine, January 1912

Index

Accidents, 57, 60, 85, 96, 117 *et seq.*, 147
Alan, Alexander, 41
Binnend, 161 *et seq.*
Bouch, Thomas, 47, 52, 63, 67 *et seq.*, 81
British Aluminium Company, 163 *et seq.*
Buccleuch, Duke of, 14, 16, 19, 21, 51
Coaches, 27, 29, 33, 43, 51, 117
Coaching, 7
Coalmasters, 60, 99, 105, 109, 111
Docks, East, 99 *et seq.*
Docks, West, 80 *et seq.*
Downie's Stables, 23
Dunfermline, 19, 20, 60, 141
Ferry, boats, 14, 39, 53, 55 *et seq*, 93, 115, 184
Ferry, crossing, 8, 10, 39, 179
Forth Bridge, 67, 70
Forth Hotel, 23, 127, 143
Gladstone, John, 14, 17, 19, 21, 51
Grainger, Thomas, 15, 20, 34, 40, 43
Granton, 11, 16, 37, 39
Hawthorn's, 27, 29, 35, 40, 64, 115
Kinghorn, 5, 8, 11, 24, 34, 45, 93, 140, 169
Kirkcaldy, 8, 11, 16, 19, 23, 94, 141
Learmonth, John, 17, 21, 27, 39
Lochgelly, 16, 19,24, 46, 61, 141
Locomotives, 29, 63, 67, 111, 117, 127, 135, 165, 174
Miller, John, 15
Napier, Robert, 23, 53
Newhaven, 10
Nicholson, Robert, 37, 40, 61

Pettycur, 8 *et seq.*, 24, 29, 34, 169
Quarries, 11, 23, 157, 159
Railway Companies
Arbroath and Forfar, 18
Caledonian, 16, 65, 67, 95
Dundee and Forfar Jn, 11
Dundee and Perth, 19
Edinburgh and Glasgow, 15, 18, 46
Edinburgh and Perth, 18, 48
Edinburgh Leith and Granton, 16, 47, 48
Edinburgh Leith and Newhaven, 15, 48
Fordell, 14, 173
Halbeath Colliery, 171
Kirkcaldy and District, 77, 94
Lancashire and Yorkshire, 63
London and North Western, 63
Manchester, Sheffield and Lincoln, 73
North British, 15, 18, 27, 65 *et seq.*, 94
Scottish Central, 20, 33, 41, 46, 52, 55
Scottish Midland Jn, 19
Scottish North Eastern, 68
St Andrews, 64
Stirling and Dunfermline, 21, 46, 60
Strathearn, 46
Wemyss and Buckhaven, 98
Russell and Macnee, 27, 43, 51
Shipbuilding, 130 *et seq.*
Stirling, John, 68, 77
Tay Bridge, 68 *et seq.*
Wagons, 29, 33, 43, 51, 61, 181
Wemyss, Randolph, 79, 98, 105

PS *William Muir* leaving Burntisland for Granton in pre-1910 condition.
Kirkcaldy Museum/1982.118

A derelict lamp stands sentinel at the West dock, now devoid of coil hoists, 1961.
J.F. McEwan/N3333